MALCOLM SAVILLE

An Illustrated Bibliography

First Edition 2014

Compiled by

Mike McGarry & Sally Walker

Cover and colour picture section (

Published

email: mystery@witchend.com

www.witchend.com

DEDICATION

This book is dedicated to Keith Richardson. He died in 2002 and generously left a legacy to The Malcolm Saville Society. After long thought, the Society decided to use this money to commission this book to benefit all its members.

First published April 2014

The authors would like to thank
the trustees of the Estate of the late Malcolm Saville
for their kind permission to use quotations.

ISBN: 978-0-9572611-2-9

Printed in the UK by Tyson Press
www.tysonpress.co.uk

Typesetting by SWATT Design Ltd
www.swatt-design.co.uk

CONTENTS

PREFACE

So let's compile a Malcolm Saville bibliography. How hard can it be? We have a start with a database produced by Guy Hawley and his team and no one is publishing Saville books at present, so no danger of it going out of date. Six months should do it.

That was in 2005. Since then we have spent countless hours on research, determined that we will include everything that is relevant and equally certain that something else will turn up the day that the proofs come back from the printers. In the meantime there has also been a mini boom in publication of Malcolm Saville's work, so producing a completely up to date bibliography is not possible.

So why did we do it? Well, first of all we said we would do it. Then, of course, it needed to be done. But the main reason was that we would enjoy putting it together. Sometimes it did not feel like enjoyment - dredging through countless editions of obscure magazines in dusty libraries, chasing up half forgotten memories from Saville fans of serials in comics whose titles eluded them or agonising over whether a particular book had different cover boards or if the sun had simply changed red to dark pink.

If you are reading this it means that we got there in the end and there are a few things we would like to tell you. First of all, this book is meant to be read, thumbed, tossed around and used. If you are a collector and want a pristine copy, buy another one and use this one. If you find something that we have got wrong then write it in (in pencil of course).

Secondly, if you like this book because it is a factual but dry tome from which you can get the information you need, then we will be disappointed. We hope you will read this book and discover that there was more to Malcolm Saville than his Lone Pine books and that there are not only Shropshire and Sussex to visit, but Yorkshire and Devon and Cumbria and London and Norfolk ....

This is not a biography of Malcolm Saville; if you would like to know more about him than we have room for here, we recommend Mark O'Hanlon's book Beyond the Lone Pine, and also membership of The Malcolm Saville Society (www.witchend.com) will get you access to its quarterly journal, where members contribute articles focussing on many areas of the author's life and works.

There will be mistakes and omissions, but not too many we hope. If you spot something, please share it with us. If there is a second edition, we will put it right. Whether you are a reader looking for paperbacks or a bibliophile aspiring to collect a complete set, we hope you enjoy this book as much as we enjoyed putting it together.

Mike and Sally (February 2014)

THANK YOU

This is the kind of book that cannot be produced without help from a great number of people; so many that the danger is someone will be missed out in any list produced. Originally we thought perhaps that we should just include a blanket thank you, but have decided to bite the bullet and name names. So our thanks to:

John Allsup	Sue Bell	Penny Cooper
Kathleen Elliott	Richard Griffiths	Ray Ham-Longman
Colin Harding	Guy Hawley	George Jasieniecki
Bernard Meade	Mark O'Hanlon	Kim Spencer
Roy Thomas	Patrick Tubby	Ian Walker

and to Steven Handy, who was a brick throughout the project

MALCOLM SAVILLE 1901 – 1982

Malcolm Saville is best known for his Lone Pine books published between 1943 and 1978, but there is so much more to his writing than that. His output included stories for children of all ages, with other series and one-off stories, plus non-fiction books which reflected his own interests and beliefs. Though not a prolific short story writer, he did produce a few, plus a number of articles, book reviews and other miscellaneous pieces, all of which get a mention in this book.

He was born in Hastings in 1901, and died there in 1982. In between he had lived in London, Hertfordshire, Surrey and several locations in Sussex. All these areas would feature in his stories, often thinly disguised. He never lived in Shropshire, though it is the county with which he was most associated and he loved it, having first visited for a holiday in 1936.

If you ask Saville devotees what distinguishes him from his contemporaries, many will mention his sense of place. Most of his books are set in real places and you know that he has been there and loved them. Many were prefaced with a foreword in which he told his young readers about the place where the story is set and let them know which of the locations they would be able to find and which they would not. In fact, he was not entirely honest here as they would be able to find virtually all the locations if they looked hard enough. So even now you can see Witchend, Seven Gates and Ingles Farm or Nettleford, Crossmarket and Ardham.

He was never a full-time writer and, for most of his writing career, held down high profile and exacting jobs, mostly in publishing. With family commitments too, writing over 90 books was a huge achievement. There was one other remarkable thing about him: starting with *Mystery at Witchend*, he included his address in his books and encouraged readers to write to him, promising each a reply. He kept this promise and we can only speculate how many thousands of letters he wrote. Additionally, there were many knocks on his door from young readers, and many lifelong fans talk of his kindness to them.

Malcolm Saville gave his young readers excitement and adventure and a lifelong love of the countryside. He encouraged friendship and loyalty. He was a very nice man.

ABOUT THIS BOOK

Our initial intention was to list editions or impressions the existence of which has been confirmed and we have stuck to this basic principle. However, it has not been easy and often a judgement has been made as to whether a book is a separate edition or just a variant. We would not expect everyone to agree with all these judgements, but in all cases these variations do get at least a mention where we have spotted them.

In the main, we have seen each book and physically compared it with other versions. Occasionally this has not been possible and we have taken the word of someone whose experience and judgement we respect. Undoubtedly there will be things we have missed and changes were made up to the date that this book was sent to the printers. We make no apologies for repeating several times that we would love you to provide details of anything that you spot which we have not.

For all the books we have started with the first published edition then listed all editions from that publisher. We then move on to the next publisher to produce the book with all further editions from them, and so on.

In all cases we have listed all information for the first edition produced by a publisher, but for subsequent editions have **only shown any changes**, with such changes being assumed to be carried forward to future editions. So, for example, if a first edition is shown with red boards and priced at 7/6 and the second edition shows the only change as a new price of 8/6, unless any amendment is shown then the next edition can be taken as having red boards and priced at 8/6.

Board colours This is a minefield. There are numerous shades of every colour. All we can say is that we have tried to be consistent and if you have a book which we have described as tan and you think it is buff or we have said mid-blue and yours seems light blue, it may be a variant but perhaps yours has just been in the sun longer than ours.

Book sizes The size is always in centimetres to the nearest ½ cm and has been obtained by simply measuring the books.

Cover scans We have included what we have and numbers in the text relate to the scan in the colour sections. Where the item was not available to us, SNA (scan not available) is shown after the number.

Editions/Impressions The original database from which this book was started was compiled by Guy Hawley and, to quote him. "In general terms an 'edition' is defined as a complete resetting of the type, whereas an 'impression' is a new printing from the existing type". So far so good but there are difficulties, not least identifying what has been done. We have used this basic principle and also tried to identify anomalies.

Of course, in many instances, the publisher tells us whether the book is an edition or impression and surely they would know what they are talking about? Well, no. There are a large number of occasions when they got it wrong, a fair number where they got it wrong the first time but corrected it in later impressions/editions and some where they got it right the first time and later corrected it to get it wrong. So we have done our best to detail what has happened and we have tried to draw attention to any anomalies, but we apologise if we have got it wrong – we are in good company!

Illustrations We have counted all illustrations, so the total shown includes vignettes, frontispieces and small pictures that may not have been included in any list of illustrations included within the books.

Illustrators Where the dustjacket/cover artist and the illustrator of the book are credited we have included their names. However there are many books where the artist is not named. This is particularly true of the Lone Pine Collins and Armada editions. It is thought that many of these were illustrated by Peter Archer who appears to have been a staff artist for Armada and was later used by Collins as a dustjacket artist.

Unfortunately we do not have space to include extra information about these artists who helped to bring Malcolm Saville's work to life but if you would like to know more about them, we would recommend John Allsup's website www.malcolmsaville.co.uk as a good starting point.

Laminated books Some Malcolm Saville hardbacks had laminated covers and these are noted in the book details. However, we have come across many more laminated books where the lamination process did not appear to have been done by the original publisher. Some were easy to spot, but others involved plenty of head scratching before we made a decision on them. In most cases this seems to have been done for libraries. One of the American editions appears with a number of different board designs and here the book appears to have been rebound in non-laminated boards. We have also come across a number of books which have 'Boots Library' embossed on the front covers and these look to have been re-bound too. In all these instances, we have not commented unless they are of particular interest.

Maps A feature of many Malcolm Saville books are the maps which are usually supposed to have been drawn by the children after their adventures. These are most commonly found at the front of the book, sometimes repeated at the back. Some have different maps at the front and back. In later editions these are often omitted, re-drawn or taken into the text of the book. Very few are credited, an exception being in *The Gay Dolphin Adventure*, where Malcolm Saville's brother David gets a credit. David Saville is known to have drawn the maps for the first three Lone Pine books, but may have done many more.

Where maps are present we have shown this in the details, but have not provided further information, unless they are of special interest. We have, however, tried to indicate when the maps are re-drawn and which version is then included in later editions. In some instances 're-drawn' means only small adjustments to the original map but, mostly, it means a completely new version has been used.

Page numbers Who would have thought this would be such a problem? We did not but, in the event, we changed our mind a number of times. Our final decision was simply to show the last numbered page, but with one exception. In a number of instances the very last page of a story has been left unnumbered. For these examples we have added one to the number of the last numbered page.

Page tinting A number of books have tinted page tops, notably Newnes and Collins Lone Pine titles. Often, but not always, the tint is a similar colour to the boards. Often, but not always, tints are only applied to the first print run of the first edition. We had intended to show the colours within the book descriptions, but it became apparent that there was inconsistency and we could not feel confident in getting it right. Unlike the boards, where the jacket might preserve the original colour, the page tops are usually unprotected and colours might fade, even disappear. Consequently, we have generally not referred to them.

Prices Normally prices are shown on dustjackets and covers and are not in dispute. However there are a number of instances where it is not so clear. A good example is Children's Book Club editions. These have no cover price but were issued with standard prices at the publication date. Some publishers used stickers which they put on the jacket and which could be changed easily. For this bibliography we have shown the price that is printed on the jacket or cover. If we know the price from another source then this is shown in brackets.

The style of the price shown in the books also varies. A pre-decimal price might be shown as 7/6 or 7s 6d or 7/6 net or something else. Post decimal books might show 60p or 60np or £0.60p. We have decided to standardise the style here. So, if the price was pre-decimal it is shown as 7/6 or 37/6. Post-decimal prices less than a pound will be shown as 60p, above a pound £3.00. If there are price variations that we know of then these are mentioned.

Proof editions Most books have corrected or uncorrected proof editions and to the collector these are often an added bonus, though expensive to acquire. Better still are copies where corrections have been noted and best of all is if those corrections have been made by Malcolm Saville.

We have seen a number of proof copies and some have features of interest. However, we do not feel that we can provide details of these as it would be impossible to provide definitive details of all the proofs that may exist.

Publication month There are reference books which list when books were published and there is other material from which dates can be obtained, but this is 'hit and miss', particularly with reprints and later editions. We thought that the neatest solution would be to leave the month out completely. However, we were conscious that the people who put our original database together had gone to some trouble over this so, in the end, we have decided to include the month where known. Interestingly, where the publication month is shown in the book, it is often quite different from when it actually appeared. So perhaps we should have kept to our original intention.

Publishers Most publishers tend to put an abbreviated version of their name on book spines and dustjackets and, generally, we have opted for this version within the bibliography. We have listed below the full names of British publishers where there are substantial differences. We have not shown those where the full name includes only the addition of 'Ltd' or 'Publishers' or similar.

Armada	Armada paperbacks, published variously by Mayfair Books Ltd, Fontana Paperbacks and William Collins Sons & Co. Ltd
Blackwell	Basil Blackwell & Mott, Ltd
Collins	William Collins Sons & Co. Ltd
Evans	Evans Brothers Ltd
Goodchild	John Goodchild Publishers
Hamlyn (Merlin)	Merlin Books, published by Paul Hamlyn Ltd
Heinemann	William Heinemann Ltd
Knight (Brockhampton)	Knight Books, a paperback division of Brockhampton Press
Mowbray	A.R. Mowbray & Co Ltd
Nelson	Thomas Nelson and Sons
Newnes	George Newnes Ltd
Scholastic (Hippo)	Scholastic Publications Ltd
Ward	Edmund Ward (Publishers) Ltd

Signed copies Malcolm Saville signed a great many books during his lifetime so they are not particularly rare. However, they do add value to books and can sometimes make them considerably more expensive. Signed copies of later books and paperbacks are the most common so look out for signed early first editions, particularly Lone Pine books.

It is rare to find books that are also signed by the illustrator; the only book where this is relatively common is *Portrait of Rye*, which is often found signed by Malcolm Saville or Michael Renton or both.

Particularly desirable are books where the signature is particularly significant. We have seen a book inscribed to 'My friend Enid Blyton' and a copy of *Jane's Country Year* dedicated to *Jane Norris*, who was the real Jane. You may also find books given to members of his family which are signed 'Uncle Len'.

SUSAN, BILL AND THE WOLF-DOG

THE LONE PINE SERIES PUBLISHED 1943-1978

The best known and best loved of Malcolm Saville's work, the Lone Pine Series was published over a period of 35 years, starting with *Mystery at Witchend* in 1943 and ending with *Home to Witchend* in 1978. The children age only gradually throughout the series, but the stories reflect the decades in which they were written and the baddies are certainly a little nastier towards the end.

The Lone Pine Club is formed in *Mystery at Witchend*, when the Morton children, David and his younger twin siblings Mary and Richard (Dickie), not forgetting their Scottie dog Macbeth (Mackie), come to live at Witchend, a house on the Long Mynd in Shropshire, while their father is away in the RAF during the war. They start the club with Petronella (Peter) Sterling, who lives with her father on the Long Mynd at Hatchholt Reservoir and Tom Ingles, another Londoner, who has been evacuated to live with his aunt and uncle at a nearby farm.

Other club members Jenny Harman and cousins Penny and Jonathan (Jon) Warrender are introduced in the subsequent two books, but the final member, Harriet Sparrow, yet another Londoner and an only child, does not appear until book ten, *Lone Pine London*. The original club rules are buried in a sardine tin beneath the pine tree in HQ1 on the Long Mynd above Witchend and club members swear an oath "to be true to each other whatever happens always". Their secret signal is a peewit call.

Although the majority of the Lone Pine stories are based in Shropshire, and usually on and around the Long Mynd, the children also have adventures in Sussex, Yorkshire, Suffolk, Dartmoor and London and all in locations which the reader can visit and enjoy. The introductions to the books detail which locations are real and which are imaginary but, as noted elsewhere in this book, many 'imaginary' locations can be found if the reader knows where to look!

Unusually perhaps, Malcolm Saville does not bring all of the members into all of the stories: only the Mortons feature in all twenty full length books, although they do not

13

appear in the only Lone Pine short story, *The Flower-show Hat*. *Home to Witchend*, the finale to the series, is the only story to feature them all, but even here they do not all take an active part in the adventure. *Home to Witchend* ties up many loose ends relating to the children's future and the future of the club; for this reason some lifelong fans have chosen not to read this final book, not wishing to believe the series has ended.

For more detailed information about the books, plots and characters, we thoroughly recommend Mark O'Hanlon's publication *The Complete Lone Pine*. Also there are many excellent articles in The Malcolm Saville Society's newsletter *Acksherley!* about all aspects of the Lone Pine series.

For a long time it seemed that even the Lone Pine series had gone out of fashion, but recent years have seen a new hardback edition of *Home to Witchend* and Girls Gone By will soon have finished publishing the complete series in paperback.

The Lone Pine books are the most collectable of Malcolm Saville's work, with high prices now being charged for first editions, particularly for the early and later titles. It is still possible however for paperback editions to be found relatively cheaply in second-hand book shops and charity shops and anyone looking for a reading set should not be put off by high prices asked by some internet sellers. It can be a very rewarding series for collectors with many editions, variations and foreign editions to collect.

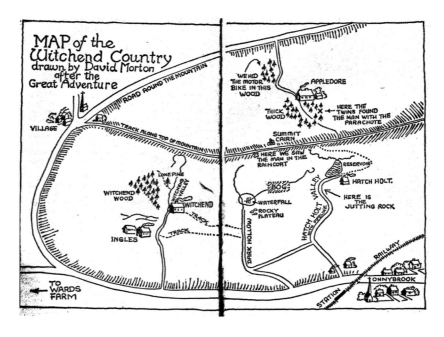

MYSTERY AT WITCHEND

"They changed trains at Shrewsbury". The first line of the first Lone Pine story and Malcolm Saville's first attempt at writing for children. His own children had been evacuated to the Shropshire hills and so had the Mortons from their home in London.

The Mortons explore the Long Mynd hill when Dickie falls into a bog and is rescued by Peter, whose father is in charge of the local reservoir. Mary finds a clearing in the forest above Witchend, the house where the Mortons stay, and it becomes their secret campsite. Tom, a London boy who has been evacuated nearby, is enrolled into the Lone Pine Club, whose aim is "exploring and watching birds and animals and tracking strangers".

The story concerns an attempt by German spies to blow up a reservoir at Hatchholt and thus disrupt the water supply to the Midlands. The children are not wholly successful in foiling this dastardly plan but play a major role in bringing the villains to justice.

In *Mystery at Witchend* the many elements which feature throughout the series are introduced: Witchend, the Lone Pine (which becomes the symbol of the club), the peewit call (which all the Lone Piners would use) and, perhaps most importantly, the Shropshire countryside. The Lone Piners would have adventures in other locations, but it was always to Shropshire where they would return.

Gretchen Breary illustrated the first edition but her pictures were soon replaced by those of Bertram Prance, and it is Prance whose illustrations are most fondly remembered and whose depictions of the Lone Piners seem to be most people's idea of what they looked like.

The first edition with original dustjacket of *Mystery at Witchend* is probably the 'holy grail' for most Saville collectors.

NEWNES Hardback 1943-1967			
First Edition 1943 (October)			**LP1**
Boards	Red	Block	Black
Pages	248	Cover price	7/6
ISBN	N/A	Size	20 x 14 cm
Abridged	No	Dustjacket	G.E. Breary
Illustrations	23 b/w	Map	Yes
Illustrator	G.E. Breary		

Second Impression 1944 (February)		
Notes	Printed on thinner paper than the first edition.	

Third Impression 1944 (August)		

Third Edition 1945		LP2
Boards	Buff	Block	Gilt
Illustrations	8 b/w	Size	19 x 12.5 cm
Illustrator	Bertram Prance	Dustjacket	Bertram Prance
Notes	A new title page vignette shows Mackie at a pool. The dustjacket now has the Prance illustration and a white spine with blue lettering (previous jackets had been wraparound).		

Fourth Edition 1946		
Boards	Tan	Block	Gilt

Fifth Edition 1948		
Boards	Tan	Block	Red
Notes	Labelled fifth edition, although the dustjacket states fourth edition and is slightly different from the real fourth jacket.		

Seventh Edition 1949		
Notes	The paper is now thicker. Labelled 7th edition, the dustjacket states fourth edition but is different from its two predecessors. There is no sixth edition.		

Eighth Edition 1950		
Notes	The jacket spine is now illustrated and shows Peter in a tree.	

Ninth Edition 1953		

Tenth Edition 1957		
Boards	Red	Block	Black

Eleventh Impression 1960		
Boards	Mid Blue	Block	Black
Cover price	8/6		

Twelfth Impression 1967		
Boards	Dark Blue	Block	Black
Cover price	10/6		
Notes	There is a variant with gold block on the spine (cover blank).		

COLLINS Hardback 1969-1971

Revised First Edition 1969		LP3
Boards	Black speckled	Block	Gilt
Pages	191	Cover price	12/6
ISBN	N/A	Size	20 x 13 cm
Abridged	Yes	Dustjacket	Not credited
Illustrations	No	Map	Yes (re-drawn)

Boards	Illustrated	Cover price	(35p) (sticker)
ISBN	0 00 160220 9	Size	18.5 x 12 cm

Notes	The illustrated cover has the same picture as was shown on the earlier Collins dustjacket. There is no discernible pattern as to which books were published by Collins in which version but, where there are both, the picture is always the same and it is often used for the Armada paperbacks too.

ARMADA Paperback 1971-1977
Revised First Edition 1971 (November)   LP4

Pages	191	Cover price	20p
Cat No	C453	Size	18 x 11 cm
Abridged	Yes	Cover	Not credited
Illustrations	No	Map	Yes (as Collins)

Revised Second Impression 1974 (March)

Cover price	25p

Revised Third Impression 1975 (November)

Cover price	40p

Revised Fourth Impression 1977

Cover price	50p

GOODCHILD Hardback 1983
Revised First Edition 1983   LP5

Boards	Light blue	Block	Gilt (spine)
Pages	210	Cover price	£5.95
ISBN	0 903445 69 7	Size	21.5 x 14 cm
Abridged	Yes	Dustjacket	Gordon King
Illustrations	No	Map	Yes (re-drawn again)

Notes	There is a variant with brown boards. At first glance the map appears to be the original Newnes version but on further examination it becomes apparent that it has been copied by another hand.

SCHOLASTIC (HIPPO) Paperback 1995
Revised First Edition 1995   LP6

Pages	295	Cover price	£3.99
ISBN	0 590 55918 4	Size	17.5 x 10.5 cm
Abridged	A few word changes	Cover	Paul Robinson
Illustrations	No	Map	Yes (re-drawn again)
Notes	The map is very similar to the Newnes version.		

GIRLS GONE BY Paperback 2006			
First Edition 2006			**LP7**
Pages	320	Cover price	(£9.99)
ISBN	1 904417 86 8	Size	19 x 13 cm
Abridged	No	Cover	G E Breary
Illustrations	G E Breary	Map	Yes (as Newnes)
Notes	The cover is a facsimile of the first edition. Both the Breary and Prance illustrations are included plus a preface by Robin Saville, a publishing history, an introduction by Mark O'Hanlon and an article by Mary Cadogan.		

MYSTERY AT WITCHEND RADIO SCRIPT

Strictly this is not an edition of *Mystery at Witchend*, but it is a book and it does have the title and Malcolm Saville's name on it, so here it is. The adaptation, for *BBC Children's Hour*, is by Barbara Sleigh: a famous name in children's radio and whilst she has included much dialogue from the original book, inevitably some is her own.

Val Biro's beautiful cover illustration was issued as a limited edition (of 30) print in 2009.

DAVID SCHUTTE Hardback 2008			
First Edition 2008			**LP8**
Boards	Burgundy	Block	Gold
Pages	128	Cover price	(£21.50/£25.00)
ISBN	978 0 9546802 5 1	Size	21.5cm x 15cm
Abridged	No	Cover	Val Biro
Illustrations	Val Biro (Frontispiece)	Map	No
Notes	One hundred copies of the book were individually numbered and signed by Val Biro and David Schutte. These were sold at £25.00. There is an introduction by Sue Bell and publisher's notes.		

SEVEN WHITE GATES

With her father away, Peter has to spend the holidays with her aunt and uncle at Seven Gates Farm on the Stiperstones in Shropshire. Whilst cycling there she first rescues a Romany girl, Fenella, whose horse has bolted and then, after a puncture, meets a new friend, Jenny Harman, who provides a lift on a cart. Peter finally makes it to the farm where she meets nice Aunt Carol and strange Uncle Micah, who badly misses his absent son Charles.

Peter persuades her aunt to let the Lone Piners come and camp in a barn at the farm (HQ2) and Jenny is invited to join. In a fast moving story, Mary and Dickie go missing, after getting up in the night to follow Uncle Micah. Despite initially being rescued by some American soldiers, they become trapped in a mine with a soldier who seems strangely familiar. The exciting cable car ride that follows is featured on the front of every edition of the book.

Newnes often got into a muddle over editions/impressions. We list what is shown in the book. Here there are two thirds and no fifth.

NEWNES Hardback 1944-1963			
First Edition 1944 (September)			**LP9**
Boards	Red	Block	Black
Pages	200	Cover price	7/6
ISBN	N/A	Size	20.5 x 14 cm
Abridged	No	Dustjacket	Bertram Prance
Illustrations	9 b/w	Map	Yes
Illustrator	Bertram Prance		
Notes	A variant has the map on the front end paper, not the inside cover.		
Second Edition 1945			
Boards	Buff	Block	Gilt
Pages	248	Size	19 x 12.5 cm
Notes	The pine tree symbol appears on the cover for the first time.		
Third Edition 1945			
Third Edition 1946			
Notes	Printed on thicker paper than the 1945 third edition.		
Fourth Edition 1948			
Boards	Buff	Block	Red

Sixth Edition 1949
Seventh Edition 1950

Notes	The jacket spine now shows Mary being lowered by a sling.

Eighth Edition 1954
Ninth Impression 1958 (June) `LP10`

Boards	Red	Block	Black	
Cover price	8/6	Dustjacket	Charles Wood	
Notes	A new dustjacket is introduced in this edition.			

Tenth Edition 1963

Cover price	10/6

COLLINS Hardback 1969-1971
Revised First Edition 1969 (October) `LP11`

Boards	Red/amber	Block	Gilt (spine)	
Pages	191	Cover price	12/6	
ISBN	N/A	Size	20 x 13 cm	
Abridged	Yes	Dustjacket	Not credited	
Illustrations	No	Map	Yes (re-drawn)	

Revised Edition 1971

Boards	Illustrated	Cover price	(35p) (sticker)	
ISBN	0 00 160222 5	Size	18.5 x 12 cm	
Notes	The cover illustration is the same as the earlier Collins dustjacket.			

ARMADA Paperback 1970-1978
Revised First Edition 1970 (October) `LP12`

Pages	191	Cover price	3/6 (17½ p)	
Cat No	C352	Size	18 x 11 cm	
Abridged	Yes	Cover	Not credited	
Illustrations	No	Map	Yes (as Collins)	

Revised Second Impression 1972 (March)

Cover price	20p

Revised Third Impression 1975

Cover price	35p

Revised Fourth Impression 1978

ISBN	0 00 690352 5	Cover price	50p

GOODCHILD Hardback 1983
Revised First Edition 1983 `LP13`

Boards	Olive Green	Block	Gilt (spine)	
Pages	190	Cover price	£5.95	
ISBN	0 903445 72 7	Size	21.5 x 14 cm	
Abridged	Yes	Dustjacket	Gordon King	
Illustrations	No	Map	No	

First Edition 2006			**LP14**
Pages	268	Cover price	(£10.99)
ISBN	1 904417 96 5	Size	19 x 13 cm
Abridged	No	Cover	Bertram Prance
Illustrations	Bertram Prance	Map	Yes (as Newnes)
Notes	The book includes a preface by Malcolm Saville's daughter, Jennifer Mettyear, an introduction by Mark O'Hanlon, an article by Mary Cadogan and an illustrated publishing history by John Allsup.		

SEVEN WHITE GATES RADIO SCRIPT

David Schutte came across the scripts for three Malcolm Saville *Children's Hour* serials whilst researching something else in a BBC archive and has faithfully re-produced them. This time the radio adaptation is by Muriel Levy and, once again, Val Biro's beautiful and evocative jacket design was issued as a print in a limited edition print of which only 30 were produced.

DAVID SCHUTTE Hardback 2009			
First Edition 2009			**LP15**
Boards	Cream	Block	Gold
Pages	128	Cover price	(£21.50/£25.00)
ISBN	978 0 9546802 9 9	Size	21.5 x 15cm
Abridged	No	Cover	Val Biro
Illustrations	Val Biro (Frontis-piece)	Map	No
Notes	One hundred copies of the book were individually numbered and signed by Val Biro and David Schutte. These were sold at £25.00. It contains an introduction by Mary Cadogan and publisher's notes and within the text are details of the cast and when the story was originally broadcast.		

THE GAY DOLPHIN ADVENTURE

This is the first book which takes the Lone Piners out of Shropshire. The Mortons go to Rye in Sussex and stay at the Gay Dolphin Hotel, owned by Mrs Warrender. They join forces with her son Jon, and niece Penny, who have encountered the villains who will become the Lone Piners' greatest enemies: Miss Ballinger, an artist, her 'niece' Valerie and Slinky Grandon. The Warrenders are later invited to join the Lone Pine Club.

In a story involving a hidden room, smugglers' treasure, kidnapping and a terribly destructive storm, the children show the resourcefulness which will become their trademark. Needless to say their enemies are roundly defeated, but they will be back.

Rye was certainly the Lone Piners' second home and four of their adventures were set in the area. Malcolm Saville knew the area well, having been born just along the coast at Hastings.

The Gay Dolphin Adventure was voted by the members of the Malcolm Saville Society as their favourite book   .

A new dustjacket was introduced in the Newnes eighth edition and this is fairly scarce, though the first edition is an even rarer bird.

NEWNES Hardback 1945-1963			
First Edition 1945 (November)			**LP16**
Boards	Tan	Block	Gilt
Pages	255	Cover price	7/6
ISBN	N/A	Size	19 x 12.5 cm
Abridged	No	Dust jacket	Bertram Prance
Illustrations	9 b/w	Map	Yes (David Saville)
Illustrator	Bertram Prance		
Second Edition 1946			
Third Edition 1948			
Boards	Tan	Block	Red
Fourth Edition 1949			
Fifth Edition 1950			
Notes	The jacket spine now has a picture of Penny looking at a map.		
Sixth Edition 1954			
Seventh Impression 1958			
Boards	Green	Block	Black
Cover price	8/6		

Eighth Impression 1963			LP17
Cover price	10/6	Dust jacket	Terence Freeman
Notes	After 18 years of Bertram Prance, a new jacket illustration was commissioned for this final Newnes impression.		

COLLINS Hardback 1969-1972

Revised First Edition 1969			LP18
Boards	Dark blue	Block	Gilt (spine)
Pages	191	Cover price	12/6
ISBN	N/A	Size	20 x 13 cm
Abridged	Yes	Dust jacket	Not credited
Illustrations	No	Map	Yes (re-drawn)
Revised Edition 1972			
Boards	Illustrated	Cover price	(45p then 50p) (stickers)
ISBN	0 00 160225 X	Size	18.5 x 12 cm
Notes	The cover is the same as the earlier Collins dustjacket.		

ARMADA Paperback 1970-1978

Revised First Edition 1970 (October)			LP19
Pages	191	Cover price	3/6 (17½ p)
Cat No	C353	Size	18 x 11 cm
Abridged	Yes	Cover	Not credited
Illustrations	No	Map	Yes (as Collins)
Revised Second Impression 1972			
Cover price	20p		
Revised Third Impression 1973			
Cover price	25p		
Revised Fourth Impression 1976			
ISBN	0 00 690353 3	Cover price	40p
Revised Fifth Impression 1978			
Cover price	50p		

GOODCHILD Hardback 1983

Revised First Edition 1983			LP20
Boards	Olive Green	Block	Gilt (spine)
Pages	225	Cover price	£6.95
ISBN	0 903445 80 8	Size	21.5 x 14 cm
Abridged	Yes	Dustjacket	Gordon King
Illustrations	No	Map	Yes (re-drawn again)
Notes	The map incorrectly labels Camber Castle as Amber Castle and the copyright date is shown as 1950.		

GIRLS GONE BY Paperback 2007			
First Edition 2007			**LP21**
Pages	310	Cover price	(£10.99)
ISBN	978 1 84745 016 6	Size	19 x 12.5cm
Abridged	No	Cover	Bertram Prance
Illustrations	Bertram Prance	Map	Yes (as Newnes)
Notes	This includes the original text but corrects some errors. It includes a publishing history and articles by Mark O'Hanlon and Mary Cadogan.		

THE GAY DOLPHIN ADVENTURE RADIO SCRIPT

This was the last of the three BBC radio scripts to be uncovered by David Schutte and completes a uniform set of three. Again, Val Biro's beautiful cover illustration was issued as a limited edition print.

The adaptor, Muriel Levy, was 'Aunty Muriel' to millions of children for, as well as adapting many stories, she appeared in some and also presented Children's Hour. She also wrote several Ladybird books.

DAVID SCHUTTE Hardback 2009			
First Edition 2009			**LP22**
Boards	Orange	Block	Gold
Pages	128	Cover price	(£21.50/£25.00)
ISBN	978 0 9544239 0 0	Size	21.5cm x 15cm
Abridged	No	Cover	Val Biro
Illustrations	Val Biro (Frontispiece)	Map	No
Notes	One hundred copies of the book were individually numbered and signed by Val Biro and David Schutte. These were sold at £25.00. It contains an introduction by Colin Harding and publisher's notes.		

THE SECRET OF GREY WALLS

The Mortons and Peter join the Witchend housekeeper, Agnes, in Clun, Shropshire to stay at her sister's guesthouse. Tom, Jenny and the Warrenders are also invited, so all the Lone Piners are together for the first time and, before the adventure ends, Jon and Penny are inducted into the club.

Some new characters are introduced: Alan Denton is a local farmer, whose sheep are going missing, and there is the mysterious Mr Cantor, who claims to be an archaeologist. There is also a re-appearance for Fenella and the other gypsies. HQ3 is established at Clun Castle and, as always, the countryside is a major character, with Offa's Dyke and a sinister house called Grey Walls featuring, as the children are let loose in a new part of Shropshire.

A new dustjacket was introduced for the sixth Newnes edition and, unusually, the 1970s Collins and Armada editions feature completely different covers. Once again, Newnes became a little confused with their editions/impressions and there is no fifth of any kind.

NEWNES Hardback 1947-1962			
First Edition 1947 (December)			LP23
Boards	Buff	Block	Red
Pages	248	Cover price	7/6
ISBN	N/A	Size	19 x 12.5 cm
Abridged	No	Dustjacket	Bertram Prance
Illustrations	8 b/w	Map	Yes
Illustrator	Bertram Prance		
Second Impression 1948			
Pages	272	Illustrations	11 b/w
Notes	This is labelled as 'reprinted' but is really a second edition as there are several changes, most notably three new Prance illustrations.		
Third Edition 1949			
Fourth Edition 1950			
Fourth Impression 1954			
Boards	Tan	Block	Red
Sixth Edition 1958 (February)			LP24
Boards	Blue	Block	Red
Cover price	8/6	Dustjacket	Charles Wood
Notes	A new jacket illustration was introduced for this edition.		
Seventh Impression 1962			
Notes	There is a variant with black block.		

HAMLYN (MERLIN) Paperback 1967-1968
Revised First Edition 1967 (October)

LP25

Pages	191	Cover price	2/6
Cat No	M21	Size	18 x 11 cm
Abridged	No	Cover	Michael Whittlesea
Illustrations	6 b/w	Map	No
Illustrator	Michael Whittlesea		

Revised Second Edition 1968

Map	Yes (re-drawn)
Notes	There is a variant with no cover price shown.

COLLINS Hardback 1972
Revised First Edition 1972

LP26

Boards	Illustrated	Block	N/A
Pages	159	Cover price	(45p) (sticker)
ISBN	0 00 160228 4	Size	18.5 x 12 cm
Abridged	Yes	Cover Illus.	Not credited
Illustrations	No	Map	Yes (re-drawn again)
Notes	The cover art is unique to this edition.		

ARMADA Paperback 1975-1979
Revised First Edition 1975

LP27

Pages	159	Cover price	35p
Cat No	C1045	ISBN	0 00 691045 9
Size	18 x 11 cm		
Abridged	Yes	Cover	Not credited
Illustrations	No	Map	Yes (as Collins)
Notes	The cover is different from the Collins edition.		

Revised Second Impression 1979

Cover price	60p

GOODCHILD Hardback 1983
Revised First Edition 1983

LP28

Boards	Grey	Block	Gilt (spine)
Pages	178	Cover price	£6.95
ISBN	0 903445 88 3	Size	21.5 x 14 cm
Abridged	Yes	Dustjacket	Gordon King
Illustrations	No	Map	Yes (re-drawn again)
Notes	The title is Secret of Grey Walls.		

SCHOLASTIC (HIPPO) Paperback 1995
Revised First Edition 1995

LP29

Pages	310	Cover price	£3.99
ISBN	0 590 55919 2	Size	17.5 x 10.5 cm
Abridged	A few word changes	Cover	Paul Robinson
Illustrations	No	Map	Yes (re-drawn again)

GIRLS GONE BY Paperback 2007
First Edition 2007

LP30

Pages	311	Cover price	(£10.99)
ISBN	978 1 84745 026 5	Size	19 x 12.5cm
Abridged	No	Cover	Bertram Prance
Illustrations	Bertram Prance	Map	Yes (as Newnes)
Notes	The book uses the original text and highlights some errors found there. It also contains a publishing history and articles by Mark O'Hanlon and Mary Cadogan.		

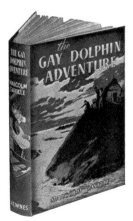

THE GAY DOLPHIN ADVENTURE

The first of the Lone Pine stories to introduce the cousins Jonathan and Penelope Warrender, who live in Rye on the edge of Romney Marsh. To this little town on its hill which once was washed by the waves of the English Channel come the Mortons, who help Jon and Penny to follow up a clue found in an old family Bible and to find a smuggler's treasure. *The Gay Dolphin* has been broadcast twice in B.B.C.'s Children Hour. 7th Impression. 8s. 6d. net.

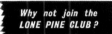

Why not join the LONE PINE CLUB?

THE SECRET OF GREY WALLS

Set in Shropshire, around the little town of Clun. Jon and Penny Warrender, from Rye, journey north to be made members of the Club and to spend part of the Christmas holidays with all the Lone Piners, including Tom Ingles and Jenny Harman. The third headquarters of the Lone Pine Club is established in the ruins of an old castle, and the members help a genial stranger to catch some sheep stealers. 6th Impression. 8s. 6d. net.

LONE PINE FIVE

Tom and Jenny meet at Bishop's Castle where Tom buys Jenny an old spoon at auction. A Mr Wilkins is interested in the spoon and he later comes to stay at the Barton Beach post office. The spoon is Roman and is not the only artefact that will feature in this story, in which the Mortons, Peter, Tom and Jenny appear.

Mr Wilkins has relations in the area, the obnoxious Mr and Mrs Smithson and their son Percy, who is kidnapped at one stage by the twins, after he throws a stone at Mackie. Smithson is a name which Malcolm Saville used a number of times, always for quite nasty folk and it is interesting that there was a shopkeeper of this name close to Malcolm Saville's home. Perhaps he was short changed by him!

Charles Sterling, now helping his father run Seven Gates Farm, comes to the rescue when the children find themselves out of their depth, literally, in a thrilling climax in a mine, with lots of water featuring.

This was the first of Malcolm Saville's book to be published in the Collins budget hardback edition, a cheap alternative to the Hamlyn paperback, which was still readily available. Their own Armada paperback would not appear for a few years. It was also the first Lone Pine story to be serialised, when it appeared in *Mickey Mouse Weekly*.

NEWNES Hardback 1949-1960			
First Edition 1949 (November)			**LP31**
Boards	Tan	Block	Red
Pages	256	Cover price	7/6
ISBN	N/A	Size	19 x 12.5 cm
Abridged	No	Dustjacket	Bertram Prance
Illustrations	9 b/w	Map	Yes
Illustrator	Bertram Prance		
Second Edition 1950			
Notes	This is really a second impression and in the lists in the two later impressions it is listed as such.		
Third Impression 1957 (June)			
Boards	Green	Block	Black
Fourth Impression 1960			
Cover price	8/6		

HAMLYN (MERLIN) Paperback 1967-1968
Revised First Edition 1967

Pages	190	Cover price	2/6
Cat No	M7	Size	17.5 x 11 cm
Abridged	No	Cover	Michael Whittlesea
Illustrations	6 b/w	Map	Yes (re-drawn)
Illustrator	Michael Whittlesea		
Notes	There is a variant with no cover price shown.		

Revised Second Edition 1968

Notes	There is a variant with no cover price shown.

COLLINS Hardback 1972
Revised First Edition 1972

Boards	Illustrated	Block	N/A
Pages	159	Cover price	(45p) (sticker)
ISBN	0 00 160230 6	Size	18.5 x 12 cm
Abridged	Yes	Cover Illus.	Not credited
Illustrations	No	Map	Yes (re-drawn again)
Notes	One version has colour paper edges at the top of the book, another doesn't and has a lighter blue panel on the top of the spine.		

ARMADA Paperback 1975-1978
Revised First Edition 1975 (November)

Pages	159	Cover price	40p
Cat No	C1060	Size	18 x 11 cm
ISBN	0 00 691060 2		
Abridged	Yes	Cover	Not credited
Illustrations	No	Map	Yes (as Collins)
Notes	The cover is different from the Collins edition.		

Revised Second Impression 1978

Cover price	60p

GOODCHILD Hardback 1984
Revised First Edition 1984

Boards	Grey	Block	Gilt (spine)
Pages	169	Cover price	£6.25
ISBN	0 86391 013 0	Size	21.5 x 14 cm
Abridged	Yes	Dustjacket	Gordon King
Illustrations	No	Map	Yes (re-drawn again)

GIRLS GONE BY Paperback 2008			
First Edition 2008			LP36
Pages	270	Cover price	(£12.00)
ISBN	978 1 84745 038 8	Size	19 x 12.5cm
Abridged	No	Cover	Bertram Prance
Illustrations	Bertram Prance	Map	Yes (as Newnes)
Notes	Also includes illustrations from other editions, publishing history and other background material.		

MICKEY MOUSE WEEKLY SERIALS

Both *Seven White Gates* and *Lone Pine Five* were serialised in *Mickey Mouse Weekly*, which ran from 1936 – 1961. The stories were much abbreviated, but both serials featured illustrations, including these simple depictions of David, Peter, Mary, Jenny, Dickie and Tom.

THE ELUSIVE GRASSHOPPER

While the events in *Lone Pine Five* are taking place, Jon and Penny are in Paris, staying with Arlette Duchelle and her family, and Jon sees someone who reminds him of their old enemy, Slinky Grandon. This is confirmed on their return to England with Arlette, when they see Grandon meet Miss Ballinger at the port. Back in Rye, Jon and Penny send the Mortons a telegram with this information. This is the only time Malcolm Saville used a link like this between two of his Lone Pine stories.

The Warrenders meet James Wilson, a journalist, who is staying at the Gay Dolphin (and who will appear in six Lone Pine books), and later find him unconscious at an abandoned school at Dungeness. Soon the Mortons are in Rye too. What is the secret of the elusive grasshoppers and what are Slinky and The Ballinger up to? Read the book to find out all.

For reasons unknown, Bertram Prance was asked to produce a new dustjacket illustration for the second impression, so out went a rather nice picture of Jon and Penny and Slinky at a Parisian café to be replaced by a scene at the beach at Dungeness. The first edition is by far the most common, but it still fetches much higher prices than later impressions.

NEWNES Hardback 1951-1966			
First Edition 1951 (September)			**LP37**
Boards	Tan	Block	Red
Pages	248	Cover price	8/6
ISBN	N/A	Size	19 x 12.5 cm
Abridged	No	Dustjacket	Bertram Prance
Illustrations	9 b/w	Map	Yes
Illustrator	Bertram Prance		
Second Impression 1954			**LP38**
Cover price	7/6		
Notes	The jacket is different from the first edition but is still by Bertram Prance. There is a variant with red boards and black block.		
Third Impression 1958			
Boards	Blue	Block	Red
Cover price	8/6		

Fourth Impression 1966

Cover price	10/6
Notes	There is a variant with blue boards and gilt block. The copyright date is incorrectly shown as 1958.

ARMADA Paperback 1965-1978
First Edition 1965 (August)   LP39

Pages	158	Cover price	2/6
Cat No	C125	Size	17.5 x 11 cm
Abridged	Yes	Cover	Peter Archer
Illustrations	6 b/w	Map	Yes (as Newnes)
Illustrator	Bertram Prance		

Second Impression 1968
New First Edition 1975 (November)   LP40

Cat No	C1046	Cover price	40p
ISBN	0 00 691046 7		
Cover	Not credited		
Notes	The cover is different from earlier Armada editions and a new foreword has also been added.		

Second Impression 1978 (December)

Cover price	60p

COLLINS Hardback 1970-1972
Revised First Edition 1970   LP41

Boards	Dark blue	Block	Gilt (spine)
Pages	185	Cover price	65p 13s.
ISBN	0 00 160207 1	Size	20 x 13 cm
Abridged	Yes	Dustjacket	Not credited
Illustrations	No	Map	Yes (re-drawn)
Notes	The book list on the rear cover includes Saucers over the Moon! The re-drawn map has a small error. The original has "Here the twins found Judith". Here she has become 'Janet'.		

Revised Edition 1972

Boards	Illustrated	Cover price	(45p) (sticker)
ISBN	0 00 160227 6	Size	18.5 x 12 cm
Notes	The cover is the same as the earlier Collins dustjacket		

GOODCHILD Hardback 1984
Revised First Edition 1984
LP42

Boards	Dark green	Block	Gilt (spine)
Pages	188	Cover price	£6.25
ISBN	0 86391 017 3	Size	21.5 x 14 cm
Abridged	Yes	Dustjacket	Gordon King
Illustrations	No	Map	Yes (as Newnes)
Notes	The copyright date is incorrectly shown as 1948.		

GIRLS GONE BY Paperback 2008
First Edition 2008
LP43

Pages	266	Cover price	(£12.00)
ISBN	978 1 84745 052 4	Size	19 x 12.5cm
Abridged	No	Cover	Bertram Prance
Illustrations	Bertram Prance	Map	Yes (as Newnes)
Notes	The book also includes illustrations from other editions, a publishing history by John Allsup and contributions from Mary Cadogan and Mark O'Hanlon.		

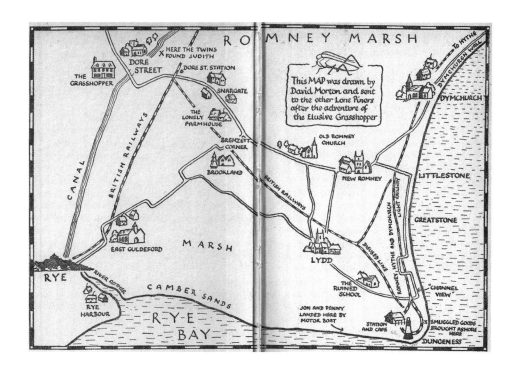

THE NEGLECTED MOUNTAIN

The Lone Piners (Mortons, Peter, Jenny and Tom) are spending the last night of the Easter holidays at Seven Gates and Charles announces his engagement to Trudie Whittington, a local vet's daughter. In the night, Peter wakes to the sound of a plane in trouble and she and David climb up to the Devil's Chair to investigate. Later, back at her home, Peter encounters two strangers, who she meets again in the summer when the adventure continues. They turn out to be two new enemies: The Doctor and John Robens.

The story involves dogs being used for experimentation and when Mackie vanishes things are not looking good, but expect him to turn up and the Lone Piners to turn up trumps. During the story the children set out in pairs to travel to the Bishop's Castle Fair and there are maps showing their various routes in all editions of the book: this is unique to this book.

The first Armada edition has an amended foreword re-titled "Older than the Ice Age" but later editions revert to the original, untitled version.

NEWNES Hardback 1953-1965			
First Edition 1953 (September)			**LP44**
Boards	Tan	Block	Red
Pages	248	Cover price	8/6
ISBN	N/A	Size	18.5 x 12.5 cm
Abridged	No	Dustjacket	Bertram Prance
Illustrations	9 b/w	Map	Yes (4)
Illustrator	Bertram Prance		
Notes	Three maps of the individual journeys are included in the text. The book has also been seen with a later sticker showing "7/6 net cheap edition".		
Second Impression 1959			
Boards	Dark blue	Block	Red
Third Impression 1965			
Boards	Lighter Blue	Block	Red
Cover price	10/6		

CHILDREN'S BOOK CLUB EDITION Hardback 1954 — LP45

Boards	Green	Block	Black (spine)
Pages	248	Cover price	(3/6)
ISBN	N/A	Size	18.5 x 12.5 cm
Abridged	No	Dustjacket	Not credited
Illustrations	9 b/w	Map	Yes (as Newnes)
Illustrator	Bertram Prance		
Notes	The jacket differs from the Newnes editions as is usually the case.		

ARMADA Paperback 1964-1978
Revised First Edition 1964 (April) — LP46

Pages	189	Cover price	2/6
Cat No	C78	Size	17.5 x 11 cm
Abridged	Yes	Cover	Peter Archer
Illustrations	9 b/w	Map	Yes (as Newnes)
Illustrator	Bertram Prance		
Notes	There is a variant with the same artwork, year and cover price but the text on page 2 is different and the advertisements at the end have been changed.		

Revised Second Edition 1969 (October) — LP47

Cat No	C295	Cover price	2/6 (12½ p)
Illustrations	8 b/w		
Notes	The cover differs from the first Armada edition and is unique to these books as, surprisingly, there is no Collins hardback edition of this title.		

Revised Third Edition 1970

Cover price	3/6 (17½ p)

Revised Fourth Edition 1971 (March)

Cover price	17½p (3/6)

Revised Fifth Edition 1973 (November)

Cover price	25p

Revised Sixth Edition 1975

Cover price	35p

Revised Seventh Edition 1978 (July)

ISBN	0 00 690195 2	Cover price	50p

GOODCHILD Hardback 1986
Revised First Edition 1986

LP48

Boards	Dark green	Block	Gilt (spine)
Pages	215	Cover price	£6.25
ISBN	0 86391 035 1	Size	22 x 14 cm
Abridged	Yes	Dustjacket	Gordon King
Illustrations	No	Map	Yes (as Newnes)
Notes	Although the illustrations were removed, the maps remain in the text.		

GIRLS GONE BY Paperback 2009
First Edition 2009

LP49

Pages	286	Cover price	(£12.00)
ISBN	978 1 84745 065 4	Size	19 x 12.5cm
Abridged	No	Cover	Bertram Prance
Illustrations	Bertram Prance	Map	Yes (as Newnes)
Notes	The book contains a publishing history by John Allsup, who also contributes a piece called Lone Pine Shropshire, which contains his own map of the area. Mark O'Hanlon and Mary Cadogan also contribute.		

LONE PINE FIVE

"Malcolm Saville is a fine story-teller."
—Children's Newspaper

The Shropshire country near the Welsh border by the mountain called the Stiperstones is called by some "The Land of Dereliction." It is wild and lonely even today, and rich in folk lore and legend. Against this sinister background the Lone Piners take part in an exciting search for Roman treasure. Peter, David, the twins and Macbeth, the Scottie, all play their part. 3rd Impression. 7s. 6d. net.

How many Lone Pine Books have you?

The ELUSIVE GRASSHOPPER

Back to Rye and Romney Marsh with Jon and Penny to the fore, in a thrilling battle of wits with their old enemies of The Gay Dolphin Adventure—"Slinky" Grandon and Miss Ballinger. The Lone Piners, their new French friend, Arlette, and a reporter from a London newspaper together solve the mystery of the antique shop called the "Grasshopper." 3rd Impression. 8s. 6d. net.

The ELUSIVE GRASSHOPPER
A LONE PINE STORY

Here is a grand way to build up your library

LONE PINE LONDON

The Mortons now live in North London and at the beginning of the Christmas holidays Jon and Penny Warrender come up to see them in their new home. No sooner have they made friends with Harriet Sparrow, whose grandfather keeps an antique shop nearby, than they are plunged into an astonishing adventure which takes them to many parts of the capital city where they must again the reporter featured in The Elusive Grasshopper. 10s. 6d. net.

WINGS OVER WITCHEND

Back to Witchend, where the Mortons come in the holidays, and Hatchholt, where Peter lives with her father about two miles away, are on the slopes of a long tableland called the Long Mynd, in Shropshire. On the top of the Mynd is a gliding station and on the eastern slopes, between steep valleys, is a new State Forest. There are Christmas tree thieves at work when this story opens and the Lone Piners are soon puzzled by the glider that is seen calling silently over the Mynd on moonlit nights. 8s. 6d. net.

Don't forget all these LONE PINE BOOKS

Here are the previous LONE PINE BOOKS

MYSTERY AT WITCHEND

The first story in the famous Lone Pine series which tells how the Morton family first came to the wild country of the Shropshire hills and found the lonely farmhouse called Witchend. Head of the astonishing adventures they found there; of how they were able to help their country to a time of peril; of how the Lone Pine Club was started and of the rules they made; of how they met Petronella ("Peter") Sterling and Tom Ingles. Has been broadcast as a play in B.B.C.'s Children's Hour. 10th Impression. 7s. 6d. net.

SEVEN WHITE GATES

Not many miles from Witchend, on the borders of Shropshire and Wales, is a gaunt and forbidding mountain called the Stiperstones, crowned with a formation of rocks known as the Devil's Chair. In the shadow of this mountain is a lonely farmhouse to which Peter is sent to visit a black-hooded uncle with a secret in his life. Has been broadcast as a play on B.B.C.'s Children's Hour. 9th Impression. 8s. 6d. net.

SAUCERS OVER THE MOOR

This is the first Lone Pine story not set in Shropshire or Sussex. The moor in the title is Dartmoor, where the children (Jon, Penny, Peter and the Mortons) stay at a country house called King's Holt with Penny's parents, who have returned to England for six months. Before they leave Rye, the Warrenders spot a flying saucer over Dungeness and meet the sinister Mr Green. Both re-appear on Dartmoor.

When Peter's bike is appropriated by Dan Sturt, a local journalist who would appear in three of their stories, the game is afoot and the Lone Piners are soon embroiled in an adventure which will see them witness an attempted assassination, help to defend their country's interests and end up being rescued by the army. The flying saucer theme was topical in 1955, as it still is today.

Goodchild editions of the Lone Pine books are riddled with errors, for example, they omitted the 'The' from *The Secret of Grey Walls*. However, their biggest error was when they changed 'Moor' to 'Moon'. This error had previously been made by Collins when listing the Lone Pine books and, even now, you often see correct editions advertised with the wrong name - saucers and moon just seem to go together!

NEWNES Hardback 1955-1963			
First Edition 1955 (September)			LP50
Boards	Buff	Block	Red
Pages	244	Cover price	8/6
ISBN	N/A	Size	19 x 12.5 cm
Abridged	No	Dustjacket	Bertram Prance
Illustrations	9 b/w	Map	Yes
Illustrator	Bertram Prance		
Second Impression 1963			
Boards	Dark Blue	Block	Black
Cover price	10/6		

CHILDREN'S BOOK CLUB Hardback 1955			LP51
Boards	Light blue	Block	Black (spine)
Pages	244	Cover price	(3/6)
ISBN	N/A	Size	19 x 12.5 cm
Abridged	No	Dustjacket	Geoffrey Whittam
Illustrations	8 b/w	Map	Yes (as Newnes)
Illustrator	Bertram Prance		

HAMLYN (MERLIN) Paperback 1967-1968
Revised First Edition 1967

LP52

Pages	192	Cover price	2/6
Cat No	M8	Size	18 x 11 cm
Abridged	No	Cover	Michael Whittlesea
Illustrations	6 b/w	Map	Yes (re-drawn)
Illustrator	Michael Whittlesea		
Notes	Variant 1 No cover price shown. Variant 2 Cover price but no 'Hamlyn' on spine.		

Revised Second Edition 1968

Notes	There is a variant with no cover price shown.

COLLINS Hardback 1972-1976
Revised First Edition 1972

LP53

Boards	Light blue	Block	Gilt (spine)
Pages	159	Cover price	80p
ISBN	0 00 160211 X	Size	20 x 13 cm
Abridged	Yes	Dustjacket	Not credited
Illustrations	No	Map	Yes (re-drawn again)

Revised Edition 1976

Cover price	£2.95

ARMADA Paperback 1976-1980
Revised First Edition 1976

LP54

Pages	159	Cover price	40p
Cat No	C1160	Size	18 x 11 cm
ISBN	0 00 691160 9		
Abridged	Yes	Cover	Not credited
Illustrations	No	Map	Yes (as Collins)
Notes	The cover illustration and map are those from the Collins editions.		

Revised Second Impression 1980

Cover price	75p	Size	17.5 x 11 cm

GOODCHILD Hardback 1984
Revised First Edition 1984

LP55

Boards	Dark Blue	Block	Gilt (spine)
Pages	177	Cover price	£6.25
ISBN	0 86391 036 X	Size	22 x 14 cm
Abridged	Yes	Dustjacket	Gordon King
Illustrations	No	Map	No
Notes	The book is incorrectly titled Saucers over the Moon and the copyright dated is shown as 1947.		

Pages	278	Cover price	(£12.00)
ISBN	978 1 84745 075 3	Size	19 x 12.5cm
Abridged	No	Cover	Bertram Prance
Illustrations	Bertram Prance	Map	Yes (as Newnes)
Notes	Includes contributions from Mary Cadogan, Mark O'Hanlon, John Allsup and Patrick Tubby.		

The NEGLECTED MOUNTAIN

The title of this book is what Jenny Harman calls the Stiperstones, under the shadow of which she lives at the village post-office and stores of Barton Beach. All the Lone Piners except Jon and Penny play a part in this exciting story, but the most dramatic part is given to their black Scottie, Macbeth. 2nd Impression.
8s. 6d. net.

... get details of the LONE PINE CLUB from your Bookseller today

SAUCERS OVER THE MOOR

Sooner or later the Lone Piners would have to become involved with something scientific and of particular interest to Jon! He hears, one moonlight night, a thin whining in the sky and *thinks* he sees a flying saucer. Then the action moves to desolate Dartmoor where the Lone Piners are staying in a lonely house taken by Penny's parents. A breathlessly exciting story set against a West Country background familiar to many readers.
8s. 6d. net.

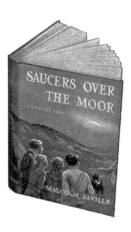

WINGS OVER WITCHEND

A gang of thieves are about but what are they stealing? Jewels? Money? No, this dastardly crew are stealing young conifers from plantations on the Long Mynd. What could they want them for? The children find out and foil the crooks.

There is no place for the Warrenders in this story, as the Mortons plan to spend Christmas at Witchend and meet up with Peter, Tom and Jenny, but the weather seems likely to scupper their plans. In a chilly adventure, the Lone Piners encounter a forest fire, a crashed glider and a pilot, Primrose Wentworth, who might be friend or foe.

Once more the descriptions of the Shropshire countryside and the real places which can be found, including the gliding club which is still there, form the backdrop to an exciting adventure.

It may appear that, with fewer hardback editions, the popularity of the Lone Pine books was waning, but this was not the case. Newnes were now confident of the success of the books and first editions were being printed in huge numbers and stocks would last for years. Soon the children's paperback would appear and Malcolm Saville's books, though abridged, would be read by an even wider audience.

This was the first book for over ten years not to be illustrated by Bertram Prance, who died soon after in 1958.

NEWNES Hardback 1956-1967			
First Edition 1956 (September)			LP57
Boards	Buff	Block	Red
Pages	247	Cover price	10/6
ISBN	N/A	Size	18.5 x 12 cm
Abridged	No	Dustjacket	Charles Wood
Illustrations	No	Map	Yes
Second Impression 1967			
Notes	There is a variant with gilt block (spine).		

ARMADA Paperback 1964-1978

Revised First Edition 1964 `LP58`

Pages	191	Cover price	2/6
Cat No	C86	Size	17.5 x 10.5 cm
Abridged	Yes	Cover	Peter Archer
Illustrations	No	Map	Yes (as Newnes)
Notes	There is a variant with a different address for Armada. The foreword has been re-written and is titled "Wild and Mysterious Country".		

Revised Second Edition 1969 (October) `LP59`

Pages	190	Cover price	2/6 (12½ p)
Cat No	C292		
Notes	The cover differs from the first Armada edition. The foreword has been re-written again and the title removed.		

Second Impression of Second Edition 1970

Cover price	3/6 (17½ p)

Third Impression of Second Edition 1971

Cover price	20p

Fourth Impression of Second Paperback Edition 1973

Fifth Impression of Second Edition 1976

ISBN	0 00 690292 8	Cover price	40p

Sixth Impression of Second Edition 1980 (January)

Cover price	70p

GOODCHILD Hardback 1986

Revised First Edition 1986 `LP60`

Boards	Black	Block	Gilt (spine)
Pages	238	Cover price	£6.95
ISBN	0 86391 037 8	Size	22 x 14 cm
Abridged	Yes	Dustjacket	Gordon King
Illustrations	No	Map	No

GIRLS GONE BY Paperback 2010

First Edition 2010 `LP61`

Pages	274	Cover price	(£12.00)
ISBN	978 184 74 50 852	Size	19 x 12.5 cm
Abridged	No	Cover	Charles Wood
Illustrations	No	Map	Yes (as Newnes)
Notes	There is an introduction to the book by John Allsup and an article by Mary Cadogan.		

LONE PINE LONDON

This is the only Lone Pine story set in London, although it is the Mortons' home city. The Warrenders are staying with the Mortons and Jon goes to White Hart Lane to watch a Spurs football match. On leaving the ground he becomes lost in the fog and calls into a shop for help. Here he meets Harriet Sparrow, who will become the twins' special friend, and she helps him to find his way.

The twins go to see Harriet at her grandfather's shop as they want to sell some old papers they found in the attic; a man immediately offers to buy them. He turns out to be an old adversary of the Lone Piners, Slinky Grandon, and wherever Slinky is then you can bet that Miss Ballinger will not be far away. There are forged paintings about and these two are certainly involved.

James Wilson makes a re-appearance and, as always, leads the children into trouble. Once more there is a kidnapping, but this time there is Harriet (and her grandfather) to help in the rescue.

The climax of the story takes place near Guildford, where Malcolm Saville lived when he wrote the book. At the very end, Harriet is invited by the twins to join the Lone Pine club, although she doesn't become an official member until *Not Scarlet but Gold*.

NEWNES Hardback 1957			
First Edition 1957 (October)			LP62
Boards	Buff	Block	Green
Pages	255	Cover price	10/6
ISBN	N/A	Size	19 x 12.5 cm
Abridged	No	Dustjacket	Charles Wood
Illustrations	1 b/w (as Newnes)	Map	Yes (2)
Illustrator	Not credited		
Notes	A variant has altered lettering for 'Newnes' on the spine. A rarer variant has green boards with red block.		

ARMADA Paperback 1965-1979			
Revised First Edition 1965 (November)			LP63
Pages	156	Cover price	2/6
Cat No	C137	Size	17.5 x 10.5 cm
Abridged	Yes	Cover	Peter Archer
Illustrations	1 b/w	Map	Yes (as 1st Newnes)
Notes	The foreword has been shortened. The second map from end of Newnes edition is missing.		

Revised First Edition 1972 (November)   `LP64`

Pages	185	Cover price	20p
Cat No	C565	Cover	Not credited
Map	Yes (re-drawn)		
Notes	The cover differs from earlier Armada editions The foreword has also been re-written.		

Revised Second Impression 1979

ISBN	0 00 690565 0	Cover price	60p

COLLINS Hardback 1970-1972
Revised First Edition 1970   `LP65`

Boards	Red	Block	Gilt (spine)
Pages	185	Cover price	65p / 13s
ISBN	0 00 160208 X	Size	20 x 13 cm
Abridged	Yes	Dustjacket	Not credited
Illustrations	No	Map	Yes (as later Armada)

Revised Edition 1972

Boards	Illustrated	Cover price	(45p) (sticker)
ISBN	0 00 160226 8	Size	18.5 x 12 cm
Notes	The cover illustration is the same as on the earlier dustjacket but the lamppost on the spine has been slightly changed.		

GOODCHILD Hardback 1986
Revised First Edition 1986   `LP66`

Boards	Dark blue	Block	Gilt (spine)
Pages	202	Cover price	£7.25
ISBN	0 86391 083 1	Size	21.5 x 14 cm
Abridged	Yes	Dustjacket	Gordon King
Illustrations	No	Map	Yes (as later Armada)
Notes	Instead of two different maps, as in the Newnes version the same, one is repeated front and back.		

GIRLS GONE BY Paperback 2010
First Edition 2010   `LP67`

Pages	284	Cover price	(£12.00)
ISBN	978 1 84745 100 2	Size	19 x 12.5 cm
Abridged	No	Cover	Charles Wood
Illustrations	No	Map	Yes (as Newnes)
Notes	There is an introduction to the book by John Allsup, an article by Mary Cadogan and a location guide by George Jasieniecki.		

What the papers said – Lone Pine series (1)

'Healthy and entertaining story' Parents' Review (MAW)

'Local legend is cleverly woven into the kind of story which all young people like' Shrewsbury Chronicle (SWG)

'A fine Yarn' Luton News (TGDA)

'The author never underestimates the intelligence of his readers' Shrewsbury Advertiser (TSOGW)

'A new standard in children's literature' Hastings Observer (LPF)

'A Rattling good story' Evening News (TEG)

'The Lone Pine Club is a fairly conventional establishment of boys and girls' Junior Bookshelf (TNM)

'A Delightful novel' London Evening News (SOTM)

'Mr Saville has once again injected life and colour into all his characters' Sussex Express (WOW)

'An absorbing book that you will not want to put down at bedtime' Nottingham Evening Post (LPL)

'A well worked-out story' The Scotsman (TSOTG)

'This is a good, racy adventure-story with plenty of suspicion and disguises' Church Times (MM)

THE SECRET OF THE GORGE

Although back in Shropshire, the Lone Piners (Tom, Jenny, Peter and the Mortons) venture further afield to the banks of the River Teme, south of Ludlow. Tom and Jenny go to a furniture sale in Ludlow with Mr Harman, where he buys a sofa from a house clearance at Bringewood Manor. Some men immediately offer to buy it from him, but he refuses and, while cleaning the sofa, Jenny finds part of an old letter hidden in it. A new friend, Nicholas Whiteflower, is living with his aunt, who used to live at Bringewood Manor, and she tells them of a diamond necklace which was stolen from the family 40 years earlier. The butler from those days, the well named Harry Sentence, has re-surfaced and he is undoubtedly up to no good. The search for the diamonds is at the heart of the story, but can anything be done before the house is pulled down?

For the first time there was no Newnes reprint, but the first edition is fairly common. The Children's Newspaper serial is well worth looking out for with its unique illustrations.

NEWNES Hardback 1958			
First Edition 1958 (September)			**LP68**
Boards	Buff	Block	Green
Pages	255	Cover price	10/6
ISBN	N/A	Size	19 x 12.5 cm
Abridged	No	Dustjacket	Charles Wood
Illustrations	1 b/w	Map	Yes (2)
Illustrator	Not credited		

CHILDREN'S BOOK CLUB Hardback 1959			**LP69**
Boards	Cream	Block	Black (spine)
Pages	255	Cover price	(3/6)
ISBN	N/A	Size	18.5 x 12.5 cm
Abridged	No	Dustjacket	Noel Syers
Illustrations	No	Map	Yes (2) (as Newnes)

HAMLYN (MERLIN) Paperback 1967-1968			
Revised First Edition 1967			**LP70**
Pages	190	Cover price	2/6
Cat No	M22	Size	18 x 11 cm
Abridged	No	Cover	Michael Whittlesea
Illustrations	6 b/w	Map	No
Illustrator	Michael Whittlesea		

Revised Second Edition 1968

Map	Yes (re-drawn)
Notes	There is a variant with no cover price.

COLLINS Hardback 1972
Revised First Edition 1972 — LP71

Boards	Illustrated	Block	N/A
Pages	159	Cover price	(45p) (sticker)
ISBN	0 00 160232 2	Size	18.5 x 12 cm
Abridged	Yes	Cover Illus.	Not credited
Illustrations	No	Map	Yes (re-drawn again)
Notes	The map is a re-drawn version of that at the front of the Newnes edition. A small spine illustration is unique to this edition.		

ARMADA Paperback 1977
Revised First Edition 1977 (May) — LP72

Pages	159	Cover price	45p
Cat No	C1328	Size	17.5 x 11 cm
ISBN	0 00 691328 8		
Abridged	Yes	Cover	Not credited
Illustrations	No	Map	Yes (as Collins)
Notes	The cover illustration and map are those in the Collins edition.		

GOODCHILD Hardback 1986
Revised First Edition 1986 — LP73

Boards	Olive green	Block	Gilt (spine)
Pages	174	Cover price	£7.25
ISBN	0 86391 084 X	Size	22 x 14 cm
Abridged	Yes	Dustjacket	Gordon King
Illustrations	No	Map	No
Notes	The original publication date is incorrectly stated as 1957. This mistake was fairly common in Goodchild books.		

GIRLS GONE BY Paperback 2011
First Edition 2011 — LP74

Pages	284	Cover price	(£12.00)
ISBN	978 1 84745 108 8	Size	19 x 12.5 cm
Abridged	No	Cover	Charles Wood
Illustrations	1 b/w (as Newnes)	Map	Yes (as Newnes)
Notes	This time, in addition to John Allsup's publishing history, there is a fascinating article by Nicholas Wood, the son of the illustrator.		

CHILDREN'S NEWSPAPER WEEKLY SERIALS

CN was published between 1919 and 1965 and at its peak sold 500,000 copies a week. vBy the 1950s it was trying to modernise and three Malcolm Saville stories were serialised, although the only Lone Pine title was (The) Secret of the Gorge, in 1958, which was the last of the three to be included. Clearly it was a highly abbreviated version but it still managed to capture the flavour of the story. Each week there was one uncredited original illustration.

A grand new Lone Pine Story

SECRET OF THE GORGE

By Malcolm Saville

There was a vicious squealing of brakes and the stranger was forced to leap for his life

Peter showed the gipsy the little whistle

MYSTERY MINE

After several changes of plan, the Lone Piners are reunited in Yorkshire (only Jenny and Tom are missing). Harriet's grandfather is buying a shop in the village of Spaunton and the children come together to investigate mysterious goings on around a mine shaft on Mr Sparrow's land, which is attracting attention. He is made an offer for the land by a stranger, Mr Warner, but he is not a stranger to Peter, who recognises him as an old foe: the same foe who they tackled in *The Neglected Mountain*, where he was the sidekick to 'The Doctor'.

It looks as if there is something in the mine which is more valuable than coal or even gold. We won't spoil the surprise but this was the height of the Cold War.

This was the second book (after *Wings over Witchend*) which had no illustrations.

NEWNES Hardback 1959			
First Edition 1959 (October)			**LP75**
Boards	Dark green	Block	Black
Pages	247	Cover price	10/6
ISBN	N/A	Size	19 x 12.5 cm
Abridged	No	Dustjacket	Terry Freeman
Illustrations	No	Map	Yes (2)
Notes	There is a variant with light green boards and gilt block and this version also sub-divides, with cover variations in the Lone Pine logo and the font for the publisher's name.		

CHILDREN'S BOOK CLUB HARDBACK 1959			**LP76**
Boards	Light blue	Block	Black (spine)
Pages	247	Cover price	(3/6)
ISBN	N/A	Size	19 x 12.5 cm
Abridged	No	Dustjacket	S.G. Mackie
Illustrations	No	Map	Yes (2)

HAMLYN (MERLIN) Paperback 1968
Revised First Edition 1968
`LP77`

Pages	189	Cover price	2/6
Cat No	M28	Size	18 x 11 cm
Abridged	No	Cover	Michael Whittlesea
Illustrations	6 b/w	Map	Yes (2) (re-drawn)
Illustrator	Michael Whittlesea		
Notes	There is a variant with no cover price.		

COLLINS Hardback 1972
Revised First Edition 1972
`LP78`

Boards	Illustrated	Block	N/A
Pages	157	Cover price	(45p) (sticker)
ISBN	0 00 160231 4	Size	18.5 x 12 cm
Abridged	Yes	Cover Illus.	Not credited
Illustrations	No	Map	Yes (re-drawn again)
Notes	A variant has a blue panel at the top of the spine, instead of purple, and the top edges of the pages are no longer tinted. Only one map appears in both the Collins and Armada editions and it is re-drawn a version of the front map from the Newnes edition.		

ARMADA Paperback 1979
Revised First Edition 1979
`LP79`

Pages	157	Cover price	60p
Cat No	C1612	Size	18 x 11 cm
ISBN	0 00 691612 0		
Abridged	Yes	Cover	Not credited
Illustrations	No	Map	Yes (as Collins)
Notes	Surprisingly, the cover illustration is different from the Collins edition.		

GOODCHILD Hardback 1986
Revised First Edition 1986
`LP80`

Boards	Brown	Block	Gilt (spine)
Pages	243	Cover price	£7.25
ISBN	0 86391 114 5	Size	21.5 x 14 cm
Abridged	Yes	Dustjacket	Gordon King
Illustrations	No	Map	No
Notes	The original copyright is incorrectly stated as 1957.		

GIRLS GONE BY Paperback 2011
First Edition 2011

Pages	280	Cover price	(£12.00)
ISBN	978 1 84745 120 0	Size	19 x 13 cm
Abridged	No	Cover	Terry Freeman
Illustrations	No	Map	Yes (as Newnes)
Notes		All change in the notes, with an introduction by Viv Turner and a publishing history by Mike McGarry, plus a short note from Peter Griffiths: one of the child models for the cover picture.	

Also available by MALCOLM SAVILLE...

JANE'S COUNTRY YEAR

This story of a girl's year spent on a farm, during which she discovers the fascinating lore of the countryside. One of the best nature books for children published for many years—now re-issued in a new format. Over 100 excellent scraperboard drawings of birds, flowers, animals, etc.   8s. 6d.

TREASURE AT THE MILL

This is an exciting new story by Malcolm Saville centred round the fascinating mill and house at Spring Valley in the Constable country of North Essex. The story itself is about treasure hidden at the mill, a secret room, an old cavalier sword and clues on an old parchment. Illustrated by Harry Pettit.   8s. 6d.

FOUR AND TWENTY BLACKBIRDS

The scene is the author's own county of Sussex and the characters, all true to life as usual, are new. It tells of the adventures of Lucinda Gray and her younger brother "Humf" when they move with their parents to the "Four and Twenty Blackbirds" cafe at Malling from the industrial Midlands.   8s. 6d.

PUBLISHED BY NEWNES

. . . order here, TODAY

To ....
.... (Bookseller)

Please supply me with the following Malcolm Saville "Lone Pine" and other books—

...... Mystery at Witchend	7s. 6d.
...... Seven White Gates	8s. 6d.
...... The Gay Dolphin Adventure	8s. 6d.
...... The Secret of Grey Walls	8s. 6d.
...... Lone Pine Five	8s. 6d.
...... The Elusive Grasshopper	8s. 6d.
...... The Neglected Mountain	8s. 6d.
...... Saucers Over the Moor	8s. 6d.
...... Wings Over Witchend	8s. 6d.
...... Lone Pine London	10s. 6d.
...... The Secret of the Gorge	10s. 6d.
...... Mystery Mine	10s. 6d.
...... Sea Witch Comes Home	10s. 6d.
...... Jane's Country Year	8s. 6d.
...... Treasure at the Mill	8s. 6d.
...... Four and Twenty Blackbirds	8s. 6d.

Name ....

Address ....

All the books described in this list are available from all Booksellers—use the handy order form on this page. In case of difficulty plus 1/- postage each from George Newnes Ltd., Tower House, Southampton Street, London, W.C.2.

Why not add an autographed Lone Pine Book to your collection this Christmas

. . . a limited number of Lone Pine Books personally autographed by Malcolm Saville are available this Christmas. Here is an exciting chance to make your collection different . . . simply order from your bookseller in the usual way at the prices shown indicating which titles you would like "Autographed". In case of difficulty simply send the list to us with a postal order for the price of the book or books plus a 1/- extra per title for postage—GEORGE NEWNES LTD., Tower House, Southampton Street, London, W.C.2. (Only books purchased now can be autographed . . . please do not send us books already in your collection).

A very Happy Christmas to You with lots of books as presents!

I have to tell you that my NEW Lone Pine adventure story won't be ready until next year but we'll write and tell you when it is. It's EXCITING!

Meanwhile, I want to remind you that there are 13 Lone Pine stories ready NOW and as I'm sure you haven't got them all these are listed for you on the next page. Any good bookshop will order any of them if you ask him right away.

Help to make this a Lone Pine Christmas by adding to your own collection of my Lone Pine books

Malcolm Saville

SEA WITCH COMES HOME

There are a number of unusual features to this book. In particular, it was the only one where the Mortons appear without the other club members. There is no doubt that Peter and Penny were very popular characters, and consequently, it is many fans' least favourite book. This is a shame because it is, possibly, the most exciting of all the Lone Pine books.

Another thing which puts people off is the quite appalling dustjacket illustration which was superimposed over a photograph that Malcolm Saville had taken himself. It is also the only book which Malcolm Saville set in Suffolk and, whilst the countryside may not be as interesting as Shropshire, the background to the story is the real life storm of 1953, which caused terrible damage to that part of the coast.

David's school friend, Paul Channing, is in trouble when his father disappears, so the Mortons accompany him to Walberswick to help him and his sister Rose. There they meet an old friend, James Wilson, who is investigating robberies of artwork painted by local artist, John Jackson. The climax of the book is the storm and such was the quality of this piece of writing that part of it was used to illustrate Malcolm Saville's work in the Eric Leyland edited *Meet your Authors*.

NEWNES Hardback 1960
First Edition 1960 (September) — LP82

Boards	Dark blue	Block	Gilt
Pages	247	Cover price	10/6
ISBN	N/A	Size	19 x 12.5 cm
Abridged	No	Dustjacket	Terry Freeman
Illustrations	No	Map	Yes (2)
Notes		The cover illustration was superimposed over a photograph taken by Malcolm Saville. There is a variant with mid blue boards and black block.	

CHILDREN'S BOOK CLUB EDITION 1961 — LP83

Boards	Blue	Block	Black (spine)
Pages	247	Cover price	(3/6)
ISBN	N/A	Size	18.5 x 12.5 cm
Abridged	No	Dustjacket	Initialled PT
Illustrations	No	Map	Yes (2) (as Newnes)

HAMLYN (MERLIN) Paperback 1968
Revised First Edition 1968
`LP84`

Pages	191	Cover price	2/6
Cat No	M27	Size	18 x 11 cm
Abridged	No	Cover	Michael Whittlesea
Illustrations	6 b/w	Map	Yes (re-drawn)
Illustrator	Michael Whittlesea		
Notes	One re-drawn map is a copy of the first Newnes map. There is a variant with no cover price.		

COLLINS Hardback 1972
Revised First Edition 1972
`LP85`

Boards	Illustrated	Block	N/A
Pages	159	Cover price	(45p) (sticker)
ISBN	0 00 160229 2	Size	18.5 x 12 cm
Abridged	Yes	Cover	Not credited
Illustrations	No	Map	Yes (re-drawn again)
Notes	A small illustration on the spine is unique to this edition.		

ARMADA Paperback 1980
Revised First Edition 1980 (January)
`LP86`

Pages	159	Cover price	70p
Cat No	C1615	Size	18 x 11 cm
ISBN	0 00 691615 5		
Abridged	Yes	Cover	Not credited
Illustrations	No	Map	Yes (as Collins)

JADE Paperback 1990
Revised First Edition 1990
`LP87`

Pages	207	Cover price	£2.99
ISBN	0 903461 36 6	Size	18 x 11 cm
Abridged	Yes	Cover	Ron King
Illustrations	No	Map	Yes (as Hamlyn)

GIRLS GONE BY Paperback 2012
First Edition 2012
`LP88`

Pages	279	Cover price	(£12.00)
ISBN	978 1 84745 134 7	Size	19 x 13 cm
Abridged	No	Cover	Terry Freeman
Illustrations	No	Map	Yes (as Newnes)
Notes	Includes an introduction by Patrick Tubby and a publishing history by John Allsup.		

A personal message to you!

My next book will be called

Sea Witch Comes Home

"Sea Witch," as you can guess, is a boat. The story is a _Lone Pine_ thriller — I think one of the most exciting I have written — and it is set in East Anglia (the bit of country shown in David's map on the other side).

Why not try and get a copy as soon as it is published? Go to your bookseller and put it on order. Or, if you like, fill in your name at the bottom of this letter and tear-off message. Then post it back to me at my publishers — George Newnes Limited, Tower House, Southampton Street, London, W.C.2.

Malcolm Saville

------- Tear Off --

Please supply a copy on publication (22nd September) of

SEA WITCH COMES HOME
(10s. 6d. net, 11s. 6d. by post)

Name ....

Address ....

The 13th Lone Pine Book . . .

NOT SCARLET BUT GOLD

As the series continued it was becoming evident that older Lone Piners are setting themselves up for romantic attachments: Peter and David, Jenny and Tom and Penny and Jon. The latter pair are, of course, first cousins. In this story the budding romance between Peter and David comes to the fore. Peter is upset because she and her father have to leave Hatchholt and because David has not written to thank her for her Christmas present, but he has written to Jenny, arranging for the Lone Piners to meet at Seven Gates. When she meets a handsome hiker, John Smith, there is jealousy in the air.

The adventure concerns a young German and his search for a hoard of money, hidden by his father during the war. In a story which features a fire, a rock fall and a kidnapping, it is Jenny who solves the 'not scarlet but gold' puzzle and brings the adventure to its conclusion.

Jon and Penny do not make it to Shropshire for this adventure, so they are not present when Harriet is made an official member of the club.

This was the only book in the series to be published by Chivers Press.

NEWNES Hardback 1962			
First Edition 1962 (September)			LP89
Boards	Red	Block	Gilt
Pages	246	Cover price	10/6
ISBN	N/A	Size	18.5 x 12 cm
Abridged	No	Dustjacket	A.R. Whitear
Illustrations	13 b/w	Map	Yes (2)
Illustrator	A.R. Whitear		
Notes	There are also four colour scene illustrations on the back of the dustjacket. There are two known variants, with silver and black block.		

CHILDREN'S BOOK CLUB EDITION 1962 `LP90`

Boards	Green	Block	Black (spine)
Pages	246	Cover price	(3/6)
ISBN	N/A	Size	19 x 12.5 cm
Abridged	No	Dustjacket	Not credited
Illustrations	13 b/w	Map	Yes (2) (as Newnes)
Illustrator	A.R. Whitear		

ARMADA Paperback 1969-1978

Revised First Edition 1969 (October) `LP91`

Pages	190	Cover price	2/6 (12½p)
Cat No	C291	Size	18 x 11 cm
Abridged	Yes	Cover	Peter Archer
Illustrations	1 b/w	Map	Yes (2) (as Newnes)
Illustrator	Not credited		
Notes	There is a new full page frontispiece but it is not credited.		

Revised First Edition (Overprint) 1970

Cover price	3/6 (17½p)

Revised Second Edition 1974 `LP92`

Cover price	30p	Cover	Not credited
Cat No	C938		
Notes	The cover differs from earlier Armada editions. The maps are the same as the Newnes edition, although the Collins edition had been published by now. The frontispiece has been retained but moved.		

Revised Third Edition 1978 (October)

Cover price	50p

COLLINS Hardback 1972

Revised First Edition 1972 `LP93`

Boards	Brown	Block	Gilt (spine)
Pages	159	Cover price	80p
ISBN	0 00 160212 8	Size	20 x 13 cm
Abridged	Yes	Dustjacket	Peter Archer
Illustrations	No	Map	Yes (re-drawn)
Notes	The jacket has similar artwork to the earlier Armada editions but the background to the lettering differs and the rock fall is emphasised. We have seen a much paler dustjacket – more yellow than gold. Only one map has been retained.		

JADE Paperback 1990
Revised First Edition 1990

Pages	189	Cover price	£2.99
ISBN	0 903461 44 7	Size	17 x 10.5 cm
Abridged	Yes	Cover	Ron King
Illustrations	No	Map	No

CHIVERS PRESS Hardback 1992
New First Edition 1992

LP95

Boards	Illustrated	Block	N/A
Pages	189	Cover price	(£8.95) (sticker)
ISBN	0 86220 891 2	Size	20 x 12.5 cm
Abridged	Yes	Cover	Not credited
Illustrations	No	Map	No
Notes	The cover is not credited but the initials RFB are visible. Mackie is white on the cover - a westie? The book is variously shown as being published by Swift, Firecrest Publishing and Chivers Press.		

GIRLS GONE BY Paperback 2012
First Edition 2012

LP96

Pages	264	Cover price	(£12.00)
ISBN	978 1 84745 143 9	Size	19 x 13 cm
Abridged	No	Cover	A.R. Whitear
Illustrations	A.R. Whitear	Map	Yes (as Newnes)
Notes	Includes an introduction by Steven Handy and a publishing history by John Allsup.		

TREASURE AT AMORYS

It had been thirteen years since the last Sussex adventure and, as usual when they are in this area, the evil Miss Ballinger puts in an appearance, but this time without her sidekick Slinky Grandon.

With the Gay Dolphin close to full and the Mortons arriving soon, Mrs Warrender suggests that the children stay at a house she has seen advertised on the Isle of Oxney, a few miles away across Romney Marsh. Jon and Penny go to look at the house, Amorys, and the owner, Major Bolshaw, agrees to let them stay. While they are there another man calls, asking to rent rooms or to buy the house, but the Major refuses. He then shows Jon and Penny the garden and tells them about the Romans who lived in the area. Penny falls asleep and dreams about a Roman temple. On their way to Amorys, Jon, Penny and the Mortons stop at an inn and are seen by Valerie, Miss Ballinger's niece. Soon they are protecting the house from would-be intruders who seem to think there is something worth finding – and there is.

After a gap of only one book, Terence Freeman was again the illustrator and, for the only time, he provided both cover and text illustrations.

From here on, all first editions are scarcer and more expensive.

NEWNES Hardback 1964			
First Edition 1964 (April)			LP97
Boards	Dark blue	Block	Gilt
Pages	192	Cover price	10/6
ISBN	N/A	Size	19 x 12.5 cm
Abridged	No	Dustjacket	Terence Freeman
Illustrations	12 b/w	Map	Yes (2)
Illustrator	Terence Freeman		
Notes	The top page edges are blue but this is absent from a variant, which also omits the gold blocking and Lone Pine logo from the front cover.		

CHILDREN'S BOOK CLUB EDITION 1964 — LP98

Boards	Green	Block	Black (spine)
Pages	191	Cover price	(3/6)
ISBN	N/A	Size	19 x 12.5 cm
Abridged	No	Dustjacket	Not credited
Illustrations	11 b/w	Map	Yes (2) (as Newnes)
Illustrator	Terence Freeman		

COLLINS Hardback 1969-1971

Revised First Edition 1969 (October) — LP99

Boards	Blue/grey	Block	Gilt (spine)
Pages	189	Cover price	12/6
ISBN	N/A	Size	20 x 13 cm
Abridged	Yes	Dustjacket	Not credited
Illustrations	No	Map	Yes (2) (re-drawn)

Revised Edition 1971

Boards	Illustrated	Cover price	(35p) (sticker)
ISBN	0 00 160221 7	Size	18.5 x 12 cm

ARMADA Paperback 1970-1978

Revised First Edition 1970 (September) — LP100

Pages	189	Cover price	3/6 (17½p)
Cat No	C354	Size	18 x 11 cm
Abridged	Yes	Cover	Not credited
Illustrations	No	Map	Yes (2) (as Collins)
Notes	The cover has the same illustration as the Collins dustjacket.		

Revised Second Impression 1972

Cover price	20p		

Revised Third Impression 1976 (January)

ISBN	0 00 690354 1	Cover price	40p

Revised Fourth Impression 1978 (January)

Cover price	50p		
Notes	The cover no longer shows 'Armada'.		

JADE Paperback 1991

Revised First Edition 1991 — LP101

Pages	192	Cover price	£2.99
ISBN	0 903461 45 5	Size	17.5 x 10.5 cm
Abridged	Yes	Cover	Ron King
Illustrations	No	Map	No

GIRLS GONE BY Paperback 2013			
First Edition 2013			LP102
Pages	247	Cover price	(£13.00)
ISBN	978 1 84745 156 9	Size	19 x 13 cm
Abridged	No	Cover	Terence Freeman
Illustrations	Terence Freeman	Map	Yes (as Newnes)
Notes	Includes an introduction by Viv Turner and a publishing history by John Allsup.		

What the papers said – Lone Pine series (2)

'Must surely rank among his best' Sheffield Telegraph (SWCH)

'I suppose Peter had to get kissed sometime, and I'm glad Mr Saville does not let this get too mushy' John O'London's (NSBG)

'We find it hard to believe that next time we visit Rye we shall not be able to take a pint at the Gay Dolphin' Sussex Life (TAA)

'The old formula is there all right but a generous dollop of tender love has been added' The Teacher (MWTF)

'I imagine there is now a new generation of young readers readily identifying with Mr Saville's attractive characters' Sussex Express (RR)

'The Lone Piners are faced this time with adventure and danger that combine to make an absorbing tale' Birmingham Mail (SAW)

'This book has all his usual pace and excitement and suspense, against the Devon background that this author knows so well' Sunday Telegraph (WMG)

'For newcomers to these well written stories the Lone Piners are a group of boys and girls who founded a secret club at an old house called Witchend in a remote valley in the Shropshire Hills. Their adventures began back in 1943 and they are still as exciting today' Bracknell News (HTW)

MAN WITH THREE FINGERS

If the Warrenders represent the southern section of the Lone Pine Club, then Tom and Jenny are the north and this is their story, as Malcolm Saville mentions in his dedication. In the course of this tale they begin to realise how much they mean to each other.

Tom is becoming bored with the farm and is persuaded by his new friend, Ned, to join him in his lorry, making a delivery to London. Some men hijack the lorry and Tom is attacked by a man with three fingers, whom he will meet again later in the story and who will give him even more problems.

Meanwhile, the Mortons, Peter and Jenny meet up at Witchend and the adventure that ensues involves a treasure hunt, in which an assortment of new characters appear, some of whom are not as they seem. Despite Tom and Jenny taking centre stage, it is the twins who take the glory.

This was the last Lone Pine title to be published by Newnes and, though you may often find the next two titles offered at higher prices, do not be fooled. This book is much rarer; there are only a few which are harder to find. In fact all editions are fairly scarce and it may be the publishers had doubts as to whether a book with this title would attract the buyers, so it was produced in lower numbers.

NEWNES Hardback 1966			
First Edition 1966 (April)			**LP103**
Boards	Green	Block	Gilt
Pages	183	Cover price	12/6
ISBN	N/A	Size	19 x 12.5 cm
Abridged	No	Dustjacket	Michael Whittlesea
Illustrations	14 b/w	Map	Yes
Illustrator	Michael Whittlesea		

COLLINS Hardback 1969-1971			
Revised First Edition 1969 (October)			**LP104**
Boards	Green	Block	Gilt (spine)
Pages	191	Cover price	12/6
ISBN	N/A	Size	20 x 13 cm
Abridged	Yes	Dustjacket	Not credited
Illustrations	No	Map	Yes (re-drawn)

Revised Edition 1971			
Boards	Illustrated	Cover price	(35p) (sticker)
ISBN	0 00 160223 3	Size	18.5 x 12 cm

ARMADA Paperback 1971-1977

Revised First Edition 1971 (November)			**LP105**
Pages	191	Cover price	20p
Cat No	C454	Size	18 x 11 cm
Abridged	Yes	Cover	Not credited
Illustrations	No	Map	Yes (as Collins)
Notes	The cover is the same as the Collins jacket.		
Revised Second Impression 1974			
Cover price	30p		
Revised Third Impression 1977			
Cover price	45p		

GIRLS GONE BY Paperback 2013

First Edition 2013			**LP106**
Pages	264	Cover price	(£13.00)
ISBN	978 1 84745 169 9	Size	19 x 13 cm
Abridged	No	Cover	Michael Whittlesea
Illustrations	Michael Whittlesea	Map	Yes (as Newnes)
Notes	Includes an introduction by Tony Gillam and a publishing history by John Allsup.		

The new sixteenth
Lone Pine adventure . . .

MAN WITH
THREE FINGERS

by
Malcolm
Saville

This exciting, fast-moving story is the sixteenth adventure of the boys and girls who call themselves the Lone Piners. Tom Ingles, now getting bored with working on his uncle's farm, gets a lift on a London-bound lorry driven on its night journey by one of his new friends. An attack on the lorry introduces the vivid, topical plot set against the author's familiar background of the Shropshire Hills. The Lone Piners soon become involved in the thrilling consequences as they gather again at Witchend for the summer holidays.

But *Man With Three Fingers* is more than a "run-of-the-mill" adventure story for boys and girls. The Lone Piners who over the years have shared so many adventures with so many readers have now, for some time, adapted themselves to the 1960s. The older members of the Club, David and Petronella and more recently Jon and Penny have discovered what they mean to each other. In this story it is the turn of Tom and his faithful Jenny to face reality and find romance, and this is what hundreds of Lone Pine fans have asked Malcolm Saville to help them do.

Man With Three Fingers is complete in itself but is as good an introduction to the series as any of the others.

A LONE PINE ADVENTURE

MAN WITH THREE FINGERS
Malcolm Saville

See overleaf for full list of other LONE PINE BOOKS

RYE ROYAL

Next door to the Gay Dolphin live an elderly couple, Dr and Mrs Flowerdew. When her husband dies, Mrs Flowerdew is left badly off, although he has left a library of books, which have been the subject of interest from a local book dealer, Roy Royal (a rare example of a Malcolm Saville pun). We soon learn that Royal has a dark past and that his interest is not just academic.

It suits everyone for the Mortons to stay at the widow's house and they are on the spot when Mrs Flowerdew finds a note, written by her husband, in which he mentions a valuable manuscript, which he has hidden. Set against the backdrop of both Rye Fawkes and Christmas, the children set out to solve the mystery, aided by old friend James Wilson and, yet again, it is the twins who are the heroes at the end.

This is the only Lone Pine book where all editions share the same cover illustration and the only one with no map. The only other illustration is a picture on the back cover of the Armada paperbacks and the Collins' spine. Neither is credited.

Girls Gone By have been re-publishing the Lone Pine books. They started with the next two and then went back to the beginning, *Rye Royal* is expected in "spring 2014" say the publishers.

COLLINS Hardback 1969-1970

First Edition 1969 (October) — LP107

Boards	Purple	Block	Gilt (spine)
Pages	191	Cover price	12/6
ISBN	N/A	Size	20 x 13 cm
Abridged	No	Dustjacket	Not credited
Illustrations	No	Map	No

Second Edition 1970

ISBN	0 00 160201 2	Cover price	65p / 13/-

ARMADA Paperback 1973-1980

First Edition 1973 (November) — LP108

Pages	191	Cover price	25p
ISBN	0 00 690725 3	Size	18 x 11 cm
Cat No	C725		
Abridged	No	Cover	Not credited
Illustrations	No	Map	No

Cover price	40p	

Cover price	80p	

GIRLS GONE BY Paperback 2014
First Edition 2014

LP109

Pages		Cover price	
ISBN		Size	19 x 13cm
Abridged	No	Cover	Not credited
Illustrations	No	Map	No
Notes	This book is scheduled for publication in 2014.		

15. **TREASURE AT AMORYS**
Jon and Penny are joined by the Mortons at the Gay Dolphin in Rye, and help to discover a Roman temple when helping a lonely old man who has befriended them. They meet some old enemies and the twins play a lively part in foiling them.

16. **MAN WITH THREE FINGERS**
Another Shropshire story. Tom, persuaded by an old friend that lorry driving will pay him better than farming, is tempted to leave Ingles. The lorry in which he is taking a trial trip is hijacked, and then his faithful Jenny and the other Lone Piners fight to keep him out of trouble, and help a friend to find a treasure.

17. **RYE ROYAL**
"Peter" comes for the first time to Rye's Gay Dolphin and helps the Warrenders and Mortons to solve the mystery of a missing Elizabethan document. The story features the famous "Rye Fawkes" Bonfire Celebrations.

18. **STRANGERS AT WITCHEND**
In this exciting story, Harriet Sparrow, the last member of the Lone Pine Club, comes to Witchend for the first time. With the twins, she befriends a runaway boy and they all become involved in a desperate adventure which culminates in the burning of a lonely cottage on the summit of the Long Mynd.

19. **WHERE'S MY GIRL ?**
The Morton twins and David, "Peter", Tom Ingles and Jenny Harman from Shropshire find themselves at "Kings Holt" on Dartmoor. The old house has been converted into a Riding School Guest House, but the Lone Piners' suspicions are soon aroused. Host and hostess are too curious......Surely some of the visitors are unusual? ......Why does the Colonel spend so much time in his workshop carving model ponies?......And what is the fish van from Plymouth really carrying? And,most important of all, what happens to "Peter" and Jenny when they fail to return from a walk in Wistmans Wood? Both David and Tom have reason to ask,"Where's my girl? ".

MALCOLM SAVILLE is a versatile and experienced writer. MYSTERY AT WITCHEND,the first Lone Pine adventure, was also the first of 75 books which he has written since. At one time in his career he was editor of a children's weekly paper, and the books he now writes prove how much he enjoys writing for young people; He also delights in 'places', travels widely and explores the setting of all his stories, the most popular series of which is undoubtedly LONE PINE.

He welcomes letters from readers about his work and will answer yours if you write to him—c/o Collins Publishers, 14 St. James's Place, London, SW1 1PF

ALWAYS LOOK FOR THE
SIGN OF THE PINE

MALCOLM SAVILLE'S Thrilling
LONE PINE Adventures now
published by Collins and Armada

THE SIGN OF THE PINE which you see above is the symbol of the LONE PINE CLUB which reminds tens of thousands of boys and girls — and their parents — of the adventures described in the Lone Pine Books by Malcolm Saville. Each of these takes place in a real part of England which can be, and often is,visited by Lone Pine readers.

There are 19 of these stories now, and as the first was published over 30 years ago, this immensely successful series is now well on the way to delight and enthrall three generations.

And this familiar sign stands not only for an exciting adventure, but also for the qualities of courage, loyalty, friendship and resource. The most important promise of the original Lone Piners was " to be true to each other whatever happens ". And so they have been. In many parts of the world today, boys and girls are founding their own Lone Pine Clubs based on these qualities.

STRANGERS AT WITCHEND

Towards the end of the series, all of the Lone Piners took turns in becoming the mainstay of a particular story. This time it is Harriet and the twins. Harriet travels to Shropshire, with the Mortons, where her grandfather is thinking of buying another antique shop. Peter's father, Mr Sterling, is now caretaker for the Mortons and he returns to Witchend to find a man with a motorbike who says he is interested in buying the house. Later, someone breaks into Witchend. Then, while camping, the twins and Harriet befriend a runaway boy, Kevin Smith, and discover a workshop used by jewellery thieves. The Lone Piners' old friend James Wilson turns up and together they hunt for the thieves.

Once more all the books share the same cover illustration and there is another small picture on the back of the Armada paperback/Collins spine. This might be a good point to lambaste Armada for their shameful omission of artists' names. Peter Archer seems to have been their principal artist in the 1960s and was surely responsible for more than the eleven Malcolm Saville titles on which he was credited. He was also responsible for some of the Collins books but the style suggests the later Armada/Collins editions were not his work.

COLLINS Hardback 1970-1971			
First Edition 1970 (October)			**LP110**
Boards	Light blue	Block	Gilt (spine)
Pages	192	Cover price	65p (13/-)
ISBN	0 00 160290 8	Size	20 x 13 cm
Abridged	No	Dustjacket	Not credited
Illustrations	No	Map	Yes
Second Edition 1971 (October)			
Cover price	75p		

ARMADA Paperback 1974-1977			
First Edition 1974			**LP111**
Pages	192	Cover price	30p
ISBN	0 00 690913 2	Size	17.5 x 11 cm
Cat No	C913		
Abridged	No	Cover	Not credited
Illustrations	No	Map	Yes (as Collins)
Second Impression 1977			
Cover price	45p		

GIRLS GONE BY Paperback 2005			
First Edition 2005			LP112
Pages	208	Cover price	(£9.99)
ISBN	1 904417 71 X	Size	19 x 13 cm
Abridged	No	Cover	Not credited
Illustrations	No	Map	Yes (as Collins)
Notes	There is a preface by Rosemary Dowler, two articles by Mary Cadogan, an introduction by Mark O'Hanlon and a brief article and publishing history by Laura Hicks. The book incorrectly states that the cover illustration is by Steven Handy.		

ARMADA BOX SET   LP113

During the 1970s, Armada issued boxed sets of Lone Pine paperbacks. The box uses the cover illustration from The Gay Dolphin Adventure on both sides. The books inside varied but two common sets were:

Mystery at Witchend, Seven White Gates,
The Gay Dolphin Adventure, Wings over Witchend,
Lone Pine London and *Man with Three Fingers*
and
The Neglected Mountain, Rye Royal, The Gay Dolphin Adventure,
Wings over Witchend, Treasure at Amorys
and *Man with Three Fingers*

We have seen boxes that vary slightly in size and shading. We have also heard of a box which contained only five books but we cannot be sure that this was not a box of six with one book missing. We do not know the selling price of any boxed set.

WHERE'S MY GIRL?

Penny's parents have bought King's Holt, on Dartmoor, to run as a pony trekking centre and they invite the Mortons, Tom and Jenny to stay. This could have been a chance for all the Lone Piners to get together for the first time but both Jon and Penny are away in France, so it does not happen. Harriet is also missing from this adventure, which sees the children on the track of smugglers; the boxes of fish are surely red herrings!

Tom falls from a combine harvester and the accident causes him to suffer memory loss. He will remember who his girl is by the end of the story and his memory will need to return, if he is to play his part in the adventure in which old friend Dan Sturt also features.

It is interesting that Tom has quite a serious accident in this story and the Mortons witness a policeman being shot. Two stories previously Tom and his friend were seriously assaulted. Malcolm Saville was accused of not changing with the times, but there is a definite increase in the violence of the stories in the thirty years since *Mystery at Witchend* was written.

The Collins and Armada editions have different cover illustrations, although they may be by the same hand. This is the only time this happens, where Collins are the original publishers, and there is also an unusual delay between the appearance of hardback and paperback.

COLLINS Hardback 1972-1976			
First Edition 1972 (November)			**LP114**
Boards	Light blue	Block	Gilt (spine)
Pages	160	Cover price	80p
ISBN	0 00 160210 1	Size	20 x 13 cm
Abridged	No	Dustjacket	Not credited
Illustrations	No	Map	Yes
Notes	The map is an amended version of that used for Saucers over the Moor.		
Second Edition 1976			
Cover price	£2.95		
Notes	The map is an amended version of that used for Saucers over the Moor. The title lettering on the second edition jacket is much brighter than on the first edition. There is a variant dustjacket with no price shown.		

ARMADA Paperback 1978-1980

First Edition 1978 (July)

Pages	160	Cover price	50p
ISBN	0 00 691474 8	Size	18 x 11 cm
Cat No	C1474		
Abridged	No	Cover	Not credited
Illustrations	No	Map	Yes (as Collins)

First (overprint) Edition 1980

Cover price	75p

GIRLS GONE BY Paperback 2005

First Edition 2005

Pages	180	Cover price	(£9.99)
ISBN	1 904417 61 2	Size	19 x 13 cm
Abridged	No	Cover	Not credited
Illustrations	No	Map	Yes (as Collins)
Notes	There is a preface by Robin Saville, an introduction by Mark O'Hanlon and an article by Mary Cadogan.		

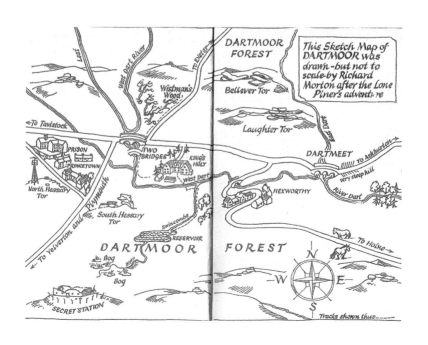

HOME TO WITCHEND

The story concerns forged banknotes, but it does not really matter. This was Malcolm Saville's chance to bring the Lone Pine saga to a close and tie up all the loose ends. By the end of the story, the six older characters would be heading for marriage and the twins and Harriet would be encouraging Kevin, Nicholas and Fenella to join them in their New Lone Pine Club. It had been six years since *Where's My Girl* and, though he left the door slightly ajar, the author surely knew that this was the end for the club.

For the only time in this series, the first edition of this book was a paperback. The Severn House hardback which followed is very rare and expensive but does not compare in quality to Richard Griffiths' 2005 version, which lovingly attempts to re-create an early Newnes edition. A Girls Gone By edition is expected in late 2014.

There is an appendix by Vivien Turner, which lists the Lone Piners and other characters, showing which books they appeared in. Appearing in this book are the nine Lone Piners, plus:

New Lone Piners: Kevin Smith, Nicholas Whiteflower and Fenella.

Relations of the Lone Piners: Albert Sparrow, Henry Harman and his wife, Alf and Betty Ingles, Mr and Mrs Morton, Jasper Sterling, Micah and Caroline Sterling, Charles and Trudie Sterling, Jack/George Warrender and his wife and Margaret Warrender.

Friends of the Lone Piners: Agnes Braid, Mr Cantor, Alan Denton, Miranda and Reuben (the gypsies), Inspector Rawlings, Johann Schmidt, Dan Sturt and James and Judith Wilson.

Enemies of the Lone Piners: Miss Ballinger, her niece Valerie and her sidekick Slinky Grandon.

Animals: Peter's pony Sally, Kevin's daschund Brock, Dolly the gypsies' horse and, of course, Mackie the Scottie dog.

ARMADA Paperback 1978-1980
First Edition 1978 (October)

Pages	159	Cover price	50p
ISBN	0 00 691477 2	Size	18 x 11 cm
Cat No	C1477		
Abridged	No	Cover	Not credited
Illustrations	No	Map	Yes
Notes	Six copies of this book were bound in hardback and given as gifts by Malcolm Saville but we do not consider this a separate edition.		

First (overprint) Edition 1980

Cover price	75p

SEVERN HOUSE Hardback 1979
New First Edition 1979 (April)

Boards	Maroon	Block	Gilt (spine)
Pages	159	Cover price	£3.50
ISBN	0 7278 0464 2	Size	20 x 13 cm
Abridged	No	Dustjacket	Not credited
Illustrations	No	Map	Yes (as Armada)
Notes	There are two variants, both with red boards, but one has no lettering on the spine.		

JADE Paperback 1990
Revised First Edition 1990

Pages	172	Cover price	£2.99
ISBN	0 903461 37 4	Size	17.5 x 10.5 cm
Abridged	No	Cover	Ron King
Illustrations	No	Map	No

RICHARD GRIFFITHS Hardback 2005
New First Edition 2005

Boards	Mid blue	Block	Red
Pages	201	Cover price	£18.00
ISBN	0 9549069 0 X	Size	18.5 x 12.5 cm
Abridged	No	Dustjacket	Anne Proctor
Illustrations	1 b/w	Map	Yes (as Armada)
Notes	The book attempts to emulate early Newnes editions in its style. There is a vignette of Mackie from The Neglected Mountain now showing an eighteenth birthday card in his mouth.		

THE FLOWER-SHOW HAT

Set in Rye, this was Malcolm Saville's only Lone Pine short story. Originally published in The Guide Gift Book in 1950, it is set between Lone Pine Five and *The Elusive Grasshopper*. It was reprinted in this form, for members of the Malcolm Saville Society, as part of the celebration of the centenary of Malcolm Saville's birth.

Only Jon and Penny appear so, for once, there are no Mortons anywhere to be seen.

A young woman, Susan Brown, comes to stay at the Gay Dolphin and Penny subsequently sees her coming out of their private rooms. Later, at a local flower show, Penny is mistaken for Susan Brown, as she has borrowed her distinctive hat.

The book was originally issued with a Society bookmark numbered between one and five. They were advertisements for the Society's activities at the time. There is a popular misconception that these are some kind of limited edition number, but there were definitely only five.

MALCOLM SAVILLE SOCIETY Hardback 2000			
Special Edition 2000			LP121
Boards	Yellow	Block	Red
Pages	31	Cover price	£18.00
ISBN	N/A	Size	19 x 13 cm
Abridged	No	Dustjacket	Kim Spencer
Illustrations	2 b/w	Map	No
Illustrator	Bertram Prance		
Notes	There is a foreword by Mark O'Hanlon and an introduction by George Jasieniecki. A variant has yellow boards and gilt block.		

THE MICHAEL AND MARY SERIES
PUBLISHED 1945-1957

Two years after the Lone Piners arrived, Malcolm Saville turned his attention to a younger audience, with the first of his stories about Michael and Mary Bishop. Throughout his writing career he would juggle series for different age groups and this clearly made sense, as his readers could move on from one series to another as they got older.

For the first time Malcolm Saville wrote a book to order. When Trouble at Townsend came out in 1945, the film of the book had already been made a year earlier, although it was not released until 1946. He had already had a book on BBC Children's Hour and now a film. His writing career had certainly started well.

Michael and Mary Bishop are townies. They live at 69 Laburnum Road in London with their mother and their Uncle Jim (her brother). Their father was killed in Normandy during the war (though he is still alive in the film). Mary is 11 and her brother two years older. They have a Scottie dog called Dougal. When we meet them, Mary is yearning for something exciting: "a fire would be fun, or perhaps an accident that wasn't too serious". She would soon get her wish in a series of fairly gentle adventures, which are set in real locations around the country.

There were seven books in the series but, uniquely for a Malcolm Saville series, there was a short story that was never published as a separate book. This was Harvest Holiday, which was a follow up to Trouble at Townsend (see The Wonder Book for Children).

TROUBLE AT TOWNSEND

In their first adventure, Michael and Mary's mother has to go to Yorkshire to look after their Granny, who is unwell, so a holiday in Clacton is cancelled. Instead, the children are sent by train and bus to stay with their Uncle Charlie at Townsend Farm at Crossmarket. Through a series of mistakes the children learn country ways and about country people, including their cousin Bob, who they initially think is a bit slow. Mike tries to ride a horse but it runs away with him; they help with  the harvest but Mike is injured, when he runs in front of the farmer shooting rabbits; Mike gets chased by a goat; Mary gets stung by bees; and they let out a cow which gets stuck in an old quarry. To cap it all there is a fire. In an interlude, Mary is given Dougal, a Scottie dog.

The story was made into a film, which included the main incidents, but there was no Dougal and the children's father had survived the war. It was filmed at Malcolm Saville's home at Westend Farm in Wheathampstead and the nearby Nomansland Common.

Lunt Roberts must have been to Westend Farm and Nomansland. The pictures can be identified, most notably The Crown and Thistle pub, which was the real life Park Hotel, now The Wicked Lady.

TRANSATLANTIC ARTS/HYPERION Hardback 1945-1947

First Hardback Edition 1945 (September)			MM1
Boards	Orange brown	Block	Purple (spine)
Pages	128	Cover price	7/6
ISBN	N/A	Size	18.5 x 12.5 cm
Abridged	No	Dustjacket	Lunt Roberts
Illustrations	21 b/w	Map	No
Illustrator	Lunt Roberts		
Notes	There is a variant with green boards and gilt block.		
Second Impression 1946 (June)			
Boards	Orange brown	Block	Blue grey (spine)
Cover price	6/-		

Boards	Brown	Block	Black

Variant 1: Pictorial boards, no dustjacket and cover price 6/-.
Variant 2: Red boards/gilt block (spine).
Variant 3: Cover price 3/6, 6/- blocked out.

Notes	It is difficult to decide who the publisher is. The jacket spine shows 'Royle', the book spine has 'Transatlantic Arts', the title page indicates 'Noel Carrington' and the rear of the jacket states 'published by Noel Carrington' and 'Transatlantic Arts distributed by Royle Publications'. You may take your choice.

JOHN MURRAY Hardback 1953
New First Edition 1953 (January)

Boards	Blue	Block	Black
Pages	128	Cover price	9/6
ISBN	N/A	Size	18.5 x 12.5 cm
Abridged	No	Dustjacket	Lunt Roberts
Illustrations	21 b/w	Map	No
Illustrator	Lunt Roberts		

Notes	The jacket illustration is a simpler version of the original. A variant with yellow boards has been seen priced at 9/6, 7/6 and 6/- so it is possible that the blue copy's price also varies.

THE RIDDLE OF THE PAINTED BOX

Uncle Jim takes Michael and Mary to Brentford to look at the canal boats on the Grand Union Canal, where they help a girl, Vicky, who is being bullied by two boys. They are then invited to take a trip on her family's boat, The Flower of Brentford. Vicky has a painted pencil box her uncle has made for her and this is attracting interest from some sinister people, but why? The children solve the mystery.

The children next feature in a story called *Harvest Holiday*, in *The Wonder Book for Children*, where they return to Townsend Farm.

ROYLE PUBLICATIONS / TRANSATLANTIC ARTS / NOEL CARRINGTON Hardback 1947

First Edition 1947 (June) — MM2

Boards	Amber	Block	Blue
Pages	164	Cover price	7/6
ISBN	N/A	Size	18.5 x 12.5 cm
Abridged	No	Dustjacket	Lunt Roberts
Illustrations	18 b/w	Map	No
Illustrator	Lunt Roberts		

JOHN MURRAY Hardback 1950-1962

New First Edition (Cheap Edition) 1950 (February)

Boards	Yellow	Block	Red
Pages	164	Cover price	5/-
ISBN	N/A	Size	18.5 x 12.5 cm
Abridged	No	Dustjacket	Lunt Roberts
Illustrations	18 b/w	Map	No
Illustrator	Lunt Roberts		

Second Impression 1953 (February) — MM3

Cover price	6/-
Notes	There is a new Lunt Roberts cover illustration.

Third Impression 1962

Boards	Light Blue	Block	Black (spine)
Cover price	9/6	Dustjacket	Lunt Roberts
Notes	There is a variant which has the title on the front boards too.		

THE FLYING FISH ADVENTURE

The children are recovering from whooping cough and go to stay with their cousin, who has a shop in Marazion, in Cornwall. While minding the shop they go to the rescue of John Shelley, who is attempting to cross the causeway from St. Michael's Mount, but has been caught by the tide. John is a runaway and soon disappears again. Who is the unpleasant woman, who comes to the shop selling a snuff box with a flying fish on it – the insignia of John's grandfather?

JOHN MURRAY Hardback 1950-1962
First Edition 1950 (October)   MM4

Boards	Light blue	Block	Red
Pages	174	Cover price	6/-
ISBN	N/A	Size	18.5 x 12.5 cm
Abridged	No	Dustjacket	Lunt Roberts
Illustrations	16 b/w	Map	No
Illustrator	Lunt Roberts		

Second Impression 1951 (January)

Boards	Blue	Block	Red

Third Impression 1955 (July)

Boards	Blue	Block	Black
Cover price	7/6		

Fourth Impression 1962 (August)

Boards	Light Blue	Block	Black
Cover price	9/6		

KNIGHT (BROCKHAMPTON) Paperback 1968-1975
Revised First Edition 1968 (October)   MM5

Pages	160	Cover price	3/6
ISBN	340 04014 9	Size	17.5 x 11 cm
Abridged	No	Cover	Not credited
Illustrations	No	Map	No
Notes	The book now contains a note from the author.		

Revised Second Impression 1975   MM6

Cover	Barry Raynor	Cover price	40p
Notes	The cover is different from the 1968 edition.		

THE SECRET OF THE HIDDEN POOL

This is Malcolm Saville's only Dorset story and the children are on holiday with their mother and Uncle Jim, in Lyme Regis. There is a mix up over accommodation but the adults are put up by some new friends, Commander and Mrs Faucett, whilst the children go camping with their new friend Billy Wright. Commander Faucett tells Michael and Mary about the Faucett treasure, which was hidden during the Civil War and could be in their old family house, which was swallowed up in a landslip 100 years earlier. Perhaps the children can help to find it.

JOHN MURRAY Hardback 1953-1962
First Edition 1953 (August) — MM7

Boards	Tan	Block	Dark Green
Pages	151	Cover price	7/6
ISBN	N/A	Size	18.5 x 12.5 cm
Abridged	No	Dustjacket	Lunt Roberts
Illustrations	15	Map	Yes
Illustrator	Lunt Roberts		

Second Impression 1962

Boards	Light blue	Block	Black
Cover price	9/6		

KNIGHT (BROCKHAMPTON) Paperback 1968-1975
Revised Edition — MM8

Pages	159	Cover price	3/6
ISBN	340 04005 X	Size	17 x 11 cm
Abridged	No	Cover	Not credited
Illustrations	1 b/w	Map	Yes (re-drawn)
Illustrator	Lunt Roberts		
Notes	There is now an end note from Malcolm Saville.		

Revised Second Impression — MM9

Cover price	40p	Cover	Barry Raynor
Notes	The cover is different from the 1968 edition.		

WHERE THE BUS STOPPED

In this story, Michael and Mary are given some money and decide to take a mystery trip to a destination they see on the front of a bus. The conductor is interested in birds and directs them to a quarry where they can do some bird watching. When they get there they help to protect the eggs of some rare birds and rescue a boy who falls over a cliff.

This book is almost legendary as the most difficult Malcolm Saville title to find. The explanation of its scarcity may be that it was published as a school reader and was not sold in any shop. A real oddity is that the three text illustrations, also on the cover, have been cut from illustrations in the earlier *The Riddle of the Painted Box*, the pictures of Michael and Dougal having been slightly altered. The book has no cover price and it was not published within the net book scheme. The prices shown are those seen in trade publications. The first edition had paper covered boards and is a different colour to later versions.

The story can also be found in the collection *Six of the Best* and the second impression page numbers (99-127) are those from that book and have been taken from run-on sheets.

BLACKWELL Hardback 1956-1966			
First Edition 1955			**MM10**
Boards	Peach	Block	Black
Pages	31	Cover price	Unknown
ISBN	N/A	Size	17.5 x 11 cm
Abridged	No	Dustjacket	No
Illustrations	3 b/w	Map	No
Illustrator	Lunt Roberts		
Notes	Publication year is shown as 1955 but it was actually April 1956.		
Second Impression 1959			
Boards	Red	Block	Black
Reprint 1964			
Reprint 1966			
Cover price	2/6		

YOUNG JOHNNIE BIMBO

Michael and Mary are staying with Vicky and travelling on The Flower of Brentford to Birmingham by canal. The engine breaks down and they have to stay at the Heart's Delight Inn for a couple of days. They visit a nearby circus and later meet Johnnie Bimbo, the son of a clown, who has run away after being wrongly accused of stealing money and poisoning the circus cats. The story centres on the circus and the children help to exonerate Johnnie and unmask the real villain.

JOHN MURRAY Hardback 1956
First Edition 1956 — MM11

Boards	Light blue	Block	Red
Pages	183	Cover price	9/6
ISBN	N/A	Size	18.5 x 12.5 cm
Abridged	No	Dustjacket	Lunt Roberts
Illustrations	20 b/w	Map	No
Illustrator	Lunt Roberts		

CHILDREN'S BOOK CLUB Hardback 1956 — MM12

Boards	Brown	Block	Black (spine)
Pages	183	Cover price	(3/6)
ISBN	N/A	Size	18.5 x 12.5 cm
Abridged	No	Dustjacket	Not credited
Illustrations	20 b/w	Map	No
Illustrator	Lunt Roberts		

KNIGHT (BROCKHAMPTON) Paperback 1970
Revised First Edition — MM13

Pages	159	Cover price	4/- (20p)
ISBN	340 04004 1	Size	17 x 11 cm
Abridged	No	Cover	Not credited
Illustrations	1 b/w	Map	No
Illustrator	Lunt Roberts		
Notes	There is a new end note from Malcolm Saville.		

THE FOURTH KEY

The Bishops are moving to Ash House in Ashfield, Sussex. The children travel down a day early and spend the night with Mrs Hobden and her son Harry. At the vicarage they meet Mr Carter, who is hoping to stay at Ash House as a paying guest. The rector tells Michael and Mary stories about smugglers who may have lived at Ash House. Harry tells them there are ghosts at Ash House and Mary and Michael go there at night when he dares them to. They see a light moving in the house and  chase a man on a bicycle. The Bishops then meet Clare, who is staying with her Aunt Peggy at nearby Rainbow Farm. Uncle Jim gives the children an old key and tells them they can have whatever it opens. The key opens a door to a secret room.

JOHN MURRAY Hardback 1957
First Edition 1957 (August) — MM14

Boards	Blue	Block	Red
Pages	182	Cover price	9/6
ISBN	N/A	Size	18.5 x 12.5 cm
Abridged	No	Dustjacket	Lunt Roberts
Illustrations	14 b/w	Map	No
Illustrator	Lunt Roberts		

CHILDREN'S BOOK CLUB Hardback 1958 — MM15

Boards	Light blue	Block	Black
Pages	182	Cover price	N/A
ISBN	N/A	Size	18.5 x 12.5 cm
Abridged	No	Dustjacket	Adrian Mapple
Illustrations	14 b/w	Map	No
Illustrator	Lunt Roberts		

KNIGHT (BROCKHAMPTON) Paperback 1970
Paperback Edition — MM16

Pages	159	Cover price	(20p) 4/-
ISBN	340 03999 X	Size	18 x 11 cm
Abridged	No	Cover	Not credited
Illustrations	1 b/w	Map	No
Illustrator	Lunt Roberts		
Notes	The book now contains a note from the author. The illustration is not credited but is the Lunt Roberts drawing from page 71 of the first edition.		

What the papers said – Michael and Mary series

'Mr Saville has written books for older children but this is a grand story for their younger brothers and sisters' Daily Mail (TAT)

'Another engaging book for children' Hastings Observer (TROTPB)

'Has a Cornish setting and is one of Malcolm Saville's best stories.... thrilling reading' Cornwall and Devon Post (TFFA)

'Told with that charm with which Malcolm Saville entrances so many junior readers' Sheffield Telegraph (TSOTHP)

'Published in April' Book News (WTBS)

'A competent piece of work but below Saville's usual standard' Worthing Gazette (YJB)

'Malcolm Saville is a lesser writer but he knows the Sussex country' Times Literary Supplement (TFK)

THE JILLIES SERIES PUBLISHED 1948-1953

Amanda 'Mandy' (16), Prudence 'Prue' (12½) and Timothy 'Tim' (11) Jillions live with their father Robert, a commercial artist, in Chelsea. Their mother is dead, and Mandy runs the household. They call their father JD (Jilly Darling). In most of the stories they are joined by Guy (17) and Mark (13) Standing, who live with their parents in the Midlands. The Standings are a 'middle class' family and their mother, in particular, does not always approve of the haphazard and somewhat bohemian lifestyle of the Jillies.

The whole series was written over a relatively short period for Malcolm Saville and the action of each of the first few books follows on from its predecessor. The characters' ages don't change over the course of the books, and, while a romance between Mandy and Guy could be assumed, they are not neatly engaged in the final book, as happens to some of the characters in other series Malcolm Saville completed in the 1970s. The Jillies were undoubtedly popular, second only to the Lone Piners in recent polls, so it is surprising they featured in only these six books.

In the Jillies books Malcolm Saville continues his tradition of setting books in real places. However, in *The Sign of the Alpine Rose*, he takes his characters abroad for the first time – to post-war Austria, when it was occupied by the British, French and Russians.

Fortunately, because the books were issued in mass produced Armada paperbacks, it is easy to find copies of all of them, although first editions can still be hard to come by. Oddly, it seems the most difficult book to find is the second edition of *Redshank's Warning*, with its new cover.

REDSHANK'S WARNING

JD and his children travel to Blakeney, Norfolk, the holiday choice of Prue, recovering from measles. They meet the Standing brothers Guy and Mark en route, and again in Blakeney, and after an inauspicious start become firm friends. Whilst exploring the area they encounter a Miss Harvey, a Mr Sandrock and Charles Martin, but are these people all they claim to be?

The children sense an adventure and pick up vital clues to solve the mystery of some stolen paintings. The adventure ends with a spectacular bonfire atop the Beacon Tower of Blakeney Church.

East Anglia is a favourite location for Malcolm Saville but he only ever set one book in each county; the Jillies visit two of them and this is the their Norfolk book. As always, he encourages his readers to visit locations in the story and Blakeney is still much as described, even today.

Unusually, the dustjacket was altered between the first and second Lutterworth editions and the latter edition is by far the harder to find.

In a members' poll, The Malcolm Saville Society found that this was the most popular of Malcolm Saville's non-Lone Pine books and the third most popular of all behind *The Gay Dolphin Adventure* and *Mystery at Witchend*.

LUTTERWORTH PRESS Hardback 1948-1954			
First Edition 1948			JS1
Boards	Blue	Block	Silver
Pages	206	Cover price	7/6
ISBN	N/A	Size	19 x 12.5 cm
Abridged	No	Dustjacket	Lunt Roberts
Illustrations	12 b/w, 1 colour	Map	Yes
Illustrator	Lunt Roberts		
Second Edition 1954			JS2
Pages	205	Dustjacket	Marcia Lane Foster
Illustrations	12 b/w		
Notes	The dustjacket is different from the first edition. The original colour frontispiece has been replaced by another of the illustrations so the page order differs from page 197 onwards. There is a variant with grey boards.		

ARMADA Paperback 1963-1970
Revised First Edition 1963

Pages	160	Cover price	2/6
Cat No	C32	Size	18 x 11 cm
Abridged	No	Cover	Charles Stewart
Illustrations	11 b/w	Map	Yes (as Lutterworth)
Illustrator	Lunt Roberts		
Notes	There is a variant which omits the cover price from the spine.		

Revised Third Impression 1970 (February)

Cat No	C310	Cover price	3/6 (17½p)
Cover	Not credited		
Notes	There is a new cover and catalogue number.		

WHITE LION Hardback 1976
New First Edition 1976 (September)

Boards	Red	Block	Gilt (spine)
Pages	205	Cover price	£2.75
ISBN	85686 174 X	Size	20 x 13 cm
Abridged	No	Dustjacket	Not credited
Illustrations	12 b/w	Map	Yes (as Lutterworth)
Illustrator	Lunt Roberts		

—this is the first of the "Jillies" books

TWO FAIR PLAITS

The Standings are spending Christmas with the Jillies. A neighbour's granddaughter, Belinda, goes missing on a train journey from Birmingham to London. The children join in the search for her, in an adventure that takes them across foggy London to Wapping and a strange new world of canals, narrow boats and wharves. The search ends when Belinda, in attempting to evade the cruel bargees who have been coerced into her abduction, is rescued from a blazing warehouse.

Although the Jillies live in London, this is the only story which is set there. A lot of the action takes place in London's docklands – an area that is much changed today, although it is still possible to find some of the locations described. The thick London fog, in which most of the adventure takes place, is also very much a thing of its time.

There is a list of illustrations at the beginning of the first edition but it omits the one on page 100. The error is repeated in every subsequent edition.

LUTTERWORTH PRESS Hardback 1948-1950			
First Edition 1948			**JS6**
Boards	Grey-blue	Block	Silver
Pages	192	Cover price	7/6
ISBN	N/A	Size	19 x 12.5 cm
Abridged	No	Dustjacket	Lunt Roberts
Illustrations	11 b/w, 1 colour	Map	Yes
Illustrator	Lunt Roberts		
Notes	An advertisement for Redshanks Warning on the back of the jacket shows the cover with a re-drawn Mandy, with long hair. A rare variant exists with brown boards/black block showing 'Askew' at the bottom of the spine, not 'Lutterworth'.		
Second Impression 1950			**JS7**
Dustjacket	Wynne		
Notes	The dustjacket is different from the first edition. There is a variant with grey boards.		

ARMADA Paperback 1966-1970
Revised First Edition 1966 (October)

Pages	159	Cover price	2/6
Cat No	C159	Size	18 x 11 cm
Abridged	No	Cover	Not credited
Illustrations	11 b/w	Map	No
Illustrator	Lunt Roberts		
Notes	There is a variant with cover price shown as 2/6 (12½p).		

Revised Second Edition 1969
Revised Third Edition 1970 (March)

Cover price	3/6 (17½p)		

WHITE LION Hardback 1977
New First Edition 1977

Boards	Deep blue	Block	Gilt (spine)
Pages	192	Cover price	£2.50
ISBN	0 85686 184 7	Size	20 x 13 cm
Abridged	No	Dustjacket	Not credited
Illustrations	11 b/w	Map	Yes (as Lutterworth)
Illustrator	Lunt Roberts		

From November 1952 to January 1953 *Two Fair Plaits* was published in *Mickey Mouse Weekly*, serialised as a picture strip and re-titled as Secret in the Mist. It was the only Malcolm Saville story to appear in this form.

STRANGERS AT SNOWFELL

Immediately after their exciting Christmas adventure, the Jillies and Standings set off by train to spend New Year in Scotland. There are several odd people on the train who intrigue the children during the journey. When the train becomes snowbound on the notorious Shap Fell and their mysterious travelling companion, Nicholas Thornton disappears, the children become involved in a chase across the snowy fell country to the sinister house called Callow. There they rescue Nicholas' father, a distinguished scientist, and highly secret documents are saved from falling into enemy hands.

The book allows Malcolm Saville to express his admiration for those who worked in the railway industry. Similar appreciation is a feature of a number of his books, and other groups which received attention were farmers, craftsmen and lifeboatmen, as well as gypsies and canal folk.

LUTTERWORTH PRESS Hardback 1949-1951			
First Edition 1949 (September)			JS10
Boards	Blue	Block	Silver
Pages	231	Cover price	7/6
ISBN	N/A	Size	19 x 12.5 cm
Abridged	No	Dustjacket	Wynne
Illustrations	12 b/w, 1 colour	Map	No
Illustrator	Wynne		
Second Impression 1951			

ARMADA Paperback 1963-1970			
Revised First Edition 1963 (February)			JS11
Pages	192	Cover price	2/6
Cat No	C22	Size	18 x 11 cm
Abridged	No	Cover	Charles Stewart
Illustrations	6	Map	No
Illustrator	Wynne		
Revised Second Edition 1967 (May)			JS12
Cat No	C178	Cover price	2/6
Cover	Peter Archer		
Notes	The cover is wrongly credited to Charles Stewart. There is a new cover and catalogue number.		
Revised Third Edition 1970 (May)			
Cover price	3/6 (17½p)		
Notes	The cover is now credited to Peter Archer.		

WHITE LION Hardback 1975			
New First Edition 1975 (August)			JS13
Boards	Blue	Block	Gilt (spine)
Pages	231	Cover price	£2.25
ISBN	85686 087 5	Size	20 x 13 cm
Abridged	No	Dustjacket	Not credited
Illustrations	12 b/w	Map	No
Illustrator	Wynne		

What the papers said – Jillies series

'A series that I am quite convinced will prove extremely popular' South London Advertiser (RW)

'Mr Saville can feel and convey the excitement of scene as well as event' John O'London (TFP)

'I regretfully note a certain slickness in action and plot, as if he found it now too easy work' Glasgow Evening Citizen (SAS)

'Occasional dash of humour' Surrey Times (TSOTAR)

'A particularly jolly good egg' Manchester Guardian (TLOS)

'Just the book to make a train journey to Scotland pass like a tuppenny bus ride' Children's Hour (TAT)

THE SIGN OF THE ALPINE ROSE

The entire family of Jillies visit Mandy's pen friend, Lisbeth, in the Austrian mountain village of Bertch, which is close to the communist occupied zone. The children are soon involved in an exciting adventure, but who is friend and who is foe and where is Lisbeth's father? JD plays a vital role in the story.

A picture of an alpine rose is missing from the illustration list in the hardback editions.

LUTTERWORTH PRESS Hardback 1950-1952
First Edition 1950 (September) · JS14

Boards	Dark green	Block	Silver
Pages	224	Cover price	7/6
ISBN	N/A	Size	19 x 12.5 cm
Abridged	No	Dustjacket	Wynne
Illustrations	13 b/w, 1 colour	Map	Yes (Gordon Randall)
Illustrator	Wynne		
Notes	There is a variant which corrects page errors in the illustration list.		

Second Impression 1952

ARMADA Paperback 1963
Revised First Edition 1963 (November) · JS15

Pages	159	Cover price	2/6
Cat No	C69	Size	18 x 11 cm
Abridged	No	Cover	Mary Gernat
Illustrations	9 b/w	Map	Yes (as Lutterworth)
Illustrator	Wynne		

WHITE LION Hardback 1976
New First Edition 1976 (November) · JS16

Boards	Dark blue	Block	Gilt (spine)
Pages	224	Cover price	£2.75
ISBN	85686 189 8	Size	20 x 13 cm
Abridged	No	Dustjacket	Not credited
Illustrations	13 b/w	Map	Yes (as Lutterworth)
Illustrator	Wynne		

THE LUCK OF SALLOWBY

In the only Malcolm Saville book to be set in Cambridgeshire, the Jillies invite the Standing brothers to stay with their Aunt Bridget in Ely. There is heavy rain and the Fens are in danger of flooding. Against this dramatic background the children discover a plot to steal the valuable 'Luck of Sallowby', a battle axe once used by Hereward the Wake, and they encounter an old enemy.

LUTTERWORTH PRESS Hardback 1952
First Edition 1952 (March) — JS17

Boards	Grey-green	Block	Silver
Pages	221	Cover price	8/6
ISBN	N/A	Size	19 x 12.5 cm
Abridged	No	Dustjacket	Not credited
Illustrations	9 b/w, 1 colour	Map	Yes (2)
Illustrator	Tilden Reeves		
Notes	Numerous variants exist: blue, grey and blue/grey boards, spines show 'Lutterworth' or 'Lutterworth Press' and occasionally maps and/or frontispieces are missing.		

ARMADA Paperback 1967
Revised First Edition 1967 (March) — JS18

Pages	190	Cover price	2/6
Cat No	C164	Size	18 x 11 cm
Abridged	No	Cover	Not credited
Illustrations	9 b/w	Map	No
Illustrator	Tilden Reeves		

WHITE LION Hardback 1976
New First Edition 1976 (July) — JS19

Boards	Green	Block	Gilt (spine)
Pages	221	Cover price	£2.50
ISBN	85686 179 0	Size	20 x 13 cm
Abridged	No	Dustjacket	Not credited
Illustrations	10 b/w	Map	Yes(2) (as Lutterworth)
Illustrator	Tilden Reeves		

THE AMBERMERE TREASURE

This is the third time that the Jillies have an adventure in a county where no other Malcolm Saville books are based. The action takes place in a fictional village, somewhere near Guildford, in Surrey. (Malcolm Saville was living in Guildford when this book was written.)

Mandy takes a holiday job looking after the niece of the Misses Anstey, the owners of 'Ambermere', a large Surrey manor house. She persuades the two sisters to open their house to the public and soon enlists her brother and sister and the Standing boys to help. They are told of hidden treasure but there are others on the trail. So who will solve the rhyming couplet clue first and discover the treasure?

This book was one of only two of Malcolm Saville's stories to be published in the USA, where it was re-titled *The Secret of the Ambermere Treasure*. It was also the only one of his books to be made into a TV series. No copy of this has surfaced and, as it was in the early days of ITV, any copies have probably been destroyed.

LUTTERWORTH PRESS Hardback 1953

First Edition 1953 (April) — JS20

Boards	Blue	Block	Silver
Pages	210	Cover price	8/6
ISBN	N/A	Size	19 x 12.5 cm
Abridged	No	Dustjacket	Marcia Lane Foster
Illustrations	7 b/w	Map	No
Illustrator	Marcia Lane Foster		

ARMADA Paperback 1963-1970

Revised First Edition 1963 (February) — JS21

Pages	192	Cover price	2/6
Cat No	C38	Size	18 x 11 cm
Abridged	No	Cover	Charles Stewart
Illustrations	No	Map	No
Notes	The foreword has been omitted.		

Revised Second Edition 1967 (May) — JS22

Cat No	C177	Cover price	2/6
Cover	Peter Archer		
Notes	The cover is wrongly credited to Charles Stewart. There is a new cover and catalogue number.		

Revised Third Edition 1969 (November)

THE BUCKINGHAMS AT RAVENSWYKE

The second book in the series is set in Whitby, in Yorkshire; a place Malcolm Saville knew well and where his son Jeremy would one day become the vicar. Charles' father is now back on the scene, but not for long; his disappearance is the start of a series of adventures, which involve a number of kidnaps, a certain amount of violence and a finale at Battersea Funfair.

There is a mysterious sailor, a mysterious scientist and a mysterious house. The children get lost on the moors in a scene that Malcolm Saville would re-enact a few years later in *Mystery Mine*. Malcolm Saville was never afraid to spin the same yarn more than once, if it was good. Keen readers might also spot plot devices from *Seven White Gates*, *The Riddle of the Painted Box* and *Susan, Bill and the Dark Stranger* in other Buckingham stories.

This is one of only two Malcolm Saville books which have been serialised both in print and on radio. The Children's Newspaper serial was published before the book, but was the only one in that publication not to have original illustrations. The BBC radio serial was the last of Malcolm Saville's books broadcast and is probably the least known.

EVANS Hardback 1952-1961
First Edition 1952 (September) BU8

Boards	Blue	Block	Gilt
Pages	216	Cover price	8/6
Cat No	Z5545	Size	19 x 13 cm
Abridged	No	Dustjacket	Alice Bush
Illustrations	11 b/w	Map	Yes (2)
Illustrator	Alice Bush		
Notes	There is a variant with the title missing from the front board.		

Second Edition 1961

Boards	Light blue	Block	Gilt (spine)
Cover price	12/6		

ARMADA (May Fair) Paperback 1968
Revised First Edition 1968 BU9

Pages	158	Cover price	2/6
Cat No	C233	Size	11 x 18 cm
Abridged	No	Cover	Peter Archer
Illustrations	No	Map	Yes (as Evans)
Notes	Though the text is not abridged, the foreword is.		

COLLINS Hardback 1971-1973
Revised First Edition 1971 BU10

Boards	Blue grey	Block	Gilt (spine)		
Pages	160	Cover price	75p		
ISBN	0 00 160602 6	Size	20 x 13.5 cm		
Abridged	Yes	Dustjacket	Peter Archer		
Illustrations	No	Map	No		
Notes	The jacket is not credited but the artwork is the same as the Armada 1968 edition. The foreword differs from Evans and Collins editions.				

Revised Second Edition 1973

Cover price	£1.50
Notes	A photograph of Malcolm Saville has been added to the rear dust-jacket flap and text on the jacket differs from the 1971 edition.

EVANS Paperback 2008
Revised First Edition 2008 BU11

Pages	216	Cover price	£5.99
ISBN	978 0 237 53569 8	Size	19.5 x 13 cm
Abridged	No	Cover	Alice Bush
Illustrations	11 b/w	Map	Yes (2) (as Evans)
Illustrator	Alice Bush		

This uncredited illustration comes from The Radio Times of 22 November 1959, to accompany an article by Malcolm Saville, to mark the first instalment of the radio serial of *The Buckinghams at Ravenswyke*.

THE LONG PASSAGE

The third Buckingham adventure is set in Sussex, Malcolm Saville's county of birth. Mr Buckingham hires a caravan and takes Juliet and Simon to stay near Brighton. It is not long before they spot an old adversary, Foxy Simmonds, and are once again plunged headlong into adventure. Charles' father is playing in a concert in Brighton and soon the three friends are together again. They meet Mr Foster, a second hand bookseller, who tells them about valuable Regency miniatures. You can bet this is not an idle conversation! Back at the campsite they meet Sarah Temple, whose mother is selling her house contents at auction the next day. Juliet and Simon bid for a box of oddments, as a keepsake for Sarah, and guess what they find in a secret drawer? A particularly good scene involves the children being chased through the bowels of The Royal Pavilion.

Unusually, the first edition is not dated (though it is known to be 26 April 1954) but the CBC copy is and shows 'reprinted 1960'.

EVANS Hardback 1954-1964

First Edition 1954 (April) — BU12

Boards	Mid blue	Block	Gilt
Pages	207	Cover price	8/6
Cat No	Z5663	Size	19 x 13 cm
Abridged	No	Dustjacket	Alice Bush
Illustrations	11 b/w	Map	Yes (2)
Illustrator	Alice Bush		
Notes	Book is undated but known to be 1954.		

Second Impression 1959

Boards	Light blue	Block	Gilt (spine)

Third Impression 1964

Boards	Mid Blue	Cover price	12/6
Map	No		
Notes	There is a different photograph of Malcolm Saville on the jacket to the first edition.		

CHILDREN'S BOOK CLUB Hardback 1960 — BU13

Boards	Red	Block	Black (spine)
Pages	207	Cover price	(3/6)
ISBN	N/A	Size	19 x 12.5 cm
Abridged	No	Dustjacket	Not credited
Illustrations	11 b/w	Map	No
Illustrator	Alice Bush		

ARMADA (May Fair) Paperback 1969-1976

Revised First Edition 1969 (February) — BU14

Pages	158	Cover price	2/6
Cat No	C260	Size	18 x 11 cm
Abridged	No	Cover	Peter Archer
Illustrations	7 b/w	Map	No
Illustrator	Alice Bush		

Revised Second Edition 1976 (January) — BU15

Cover price	40p	Cover	Gordon King
Cat No	C1166	ISBN	0 00 691166 8

EVANS Paperback 2008

Revised First Edition 2008 — BU16

Pages	207	Cover price	£5.99
ISBN	978 0 237 53570 4	Size	19.5 x 13 cm
Abridged	No	Cover	Alice Bush
Illustrations	11 b/w	Map	Yes (1) (as Evans)
Illustrator	Alice Bush		

What the papers said – Buckinghams series

'Well written story by a friendly author' Bristol Evening Post (TMOM)

'For sheer excitement there is little to beat a spy theme, especially when the storyteller is Malcolm Saville' The Scotsman (TBAR)

'You will enjoy every word of this book' Cork Examiner (TLP)

'For early teenage readers' Hull Daily Mail (APFTB)

'Compulsive reading' Oxford Mail (TSOTVR)

'The plot is both clever and exciting and the book is a real thriller' Ken Branagh (yes him!) aged 14 in The Reading Paper (DITS)

A PALACE FOR THE BUCKINGHAMS

Many Malcolm Saville characters visit London for at least one adventure and now it is the Buckinghams' turn; however the story ends in another favourite Saville location, the South Downs near Lewes. In this story Juliet and Simon are in London to stay with Uncle Joe, an artist. They meet Sir John Villiers, a famous portrait painter, who wishes to paint them, and he invites the Buckinghams to his old house on Hampstead Heath. Coincidentally Charles reads a letter from Juliet aloud, while on a flight, and is overheard by a curious stranger, who turns out to be Sir John's stepson. The story features missing treasure (again) but there is great drama, with a masked ball, a fire and a thrilling ending.

It had been nine years since the previous Buckinghams book so it would have been read by a new generation of children. This lack of continuity possibly hit sales and there were only two editions.

EVANS Hardback 1963
First Edition 1963 (May) — BU17

Boards	Grey	Block	Gilt (spine)
Pages	189	Cover price	12/6
Cat No	7/5759	Size	19 x 13 cm
Abridged	No	Dustjacket	Alice Bush
Illustrations	9 b/w	Map	No
Illustrator	Alice Bush		
Notes	There are variants with light blue and mid blue boards.		

ARMADA (May Fair) Paperback 1969
Revised First Edition 1969 (August) — BU18

Pages	158	Cover price	2/6
Cat No	C287	Size	18 x 11 cm
Abridged	No	Cover	Peter Archer
Illustrations	8 b/w	Map	No
Illustrator	Alice Bush		

THE SECRET OF THE VILLA ROSA

During the 1970s Malcolm Saville began to take his characters abroad (most notably in the Marston Baines series). In the fifth Buckingham adventure, Uncle Joe invites Juliet, Simon and Charles to stay with him at The Villa Rosa, a hotel in Orvieto, Italy, where he has been invited to paint some murals. Whilst visiting an art gallery in Florence, Joe notices a fake painting and the Buckinghams meet some Americans and later find that they too are guests at The Villa Rosa. After finding an injured man, who then disappears, and being unceremoniously ejected from the hotel, our heroes become involved in an adventure, which puts them in the clutches of a criminal gang.

Another eight years had passed since the previous book and this may have been a reason why there was no paperback edition. What is odd though is that the first edition is incredibly easy to find, which suggests a big print run and yet a second edition was produced. Collins were now the publishers and the book is uniform with the later Lone Pines and, like them, has no illustrations.

Given the limited success of this book it is surprising that this is the only Malcolm Saville title currently available as a talking book from the Royal National Institute for the Blind.

COLLINS Hardback 1971-1973			
First Edition 1971 (October)			BU19
Boards	Blue	Block	Gilt (spine)
Pages	157	Cover price	75p
ISBN	0 00 160603 4	Size	20 x 13.5 cm
Abridged	No	Dustjacket	Not credited
Illustrations	No	Map	No
Second Edition 1973			
Cover price	(£1.50) (sticker)		
Notes	The jacket is slightly different: it now has a photograph of Malcolm Saville and some amended text.		

DIAMOND IN THE SKY

In their final adventure, the Buckingham family are going to stay in Amsterdam with publisher Pieter van der Straat and his step-daughter Carla, while their father gets background material for his new book. And guess what? - the Renislau family will also be in Amsterdam as Mr Renislau is conducting some concerts. On the plane they meet Jean Smart, who is interested in a package which Juliet has dropped by accident. You may not be surprised to find that, as this is Amsterdam, diamond smuggling is on the agenda and Jean turns out to be a British Customs officer. Somebody else has an 'unbalanced personality', but we won't tell you who. You will have to read the book.

This is an enjoyable farewell to The Buckinghams. During their twenty years of adventures they had shared a lot together and fans of the series will wonder what might have happened, as there was romance in the air, with Juliet and Charles even discussing engagement.

Again, there was no paperback edition of this book and only one hardback edition. Consequently the book is comparatively rare and good quality editions with dustjackets can be very expensive.

The book is unique amongst all Malcolm Saville's Collins' editions in having maps at the front and back partly on the inside cover. In other books they were on inside pages and in some cases, where they were not the original publisher, they omitted them.

COLLINS Hardback 1974			
First Edition 1974 (November)			BU20
Boards	Blue-grey	Block	Gilt (spine)
Pages	158	Cover price	(£1.50) (sticker)
ISBN	0 00 160604 2	Size	20 x 13.5 cm
Abridged	No	Dustjacket	Not credited
Illustrations	No	Map	Yes

  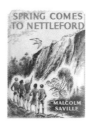 

Many contemporary reviews of these books call it a 'family series'. What they probably mean is the stories are gentler than in some of Malcolm Saville's other books, often a series of small incidents, rather than a big adventure leading to a climax. Perhaps this was not popular with readers and thus the series ended after only four books, although maybe the plan was always to follow the characters through only one year.

Unusually for Malcolm Saville, Nettleford is a fictional village although there are references to Malcolm Saville's home at Westend Farm. The Nicky Line (SCTN) is real and Northend Farm appears in three of the books. The maps do not help and our best suggestion is that Nettleford has elements of Harpenden and Hemel Hempstead Old Town.

The main family are the Richardsons: Sally, Paul and Veronica (Vee), who live at the Wise Owl Bookshop with their parents. Sharing their adventures are Elizabeth (Liz, Liza, Lizbeth) Langton, who lives with her parents and two brothers (Charles and Hugh) at the local vicarage, and Jimmy Brand, the ironmonger's son. Of course, they form a secret society, The Owlers, though there is a mention of an earlier society called The Peewits! Other important characters are the Wilkins, at Northend Farm, and Miss Phelps (Phelpy), who works at the bookshop. The first three stories take place in Nettleford, with the fourth, *The Secret of Buzzard Scar*, being set in Yorkshire.

If you are interested in the Nettleford series we recommend Rowena Edlin-White's article *Nettleford Revisited* in *Acksherley!* number 14.

ALL SUMMER THROUGH

The book introduces us to the main characters, Sally, Paul, Elizabeth and Jimmy, and they form a club: The Owlers. Mrs Richardson is asked to look after her stuck-up nephew, Tony, for three weeks during the summer holidays and eventually Tony proves his worth and is allowed to join the club. The children go to nearby Northend Farm (Malcolm Saville's previous home was Westend Farm) to camp, where they assist in bringing in the harvest and help when fire is discovered. The children then organise a party for two lonely invalids. Later in the story the Richardsons and Tony go off to Tenby for a holiday, where they rescue a boy, who has been blown over a cliff.

This is not a difficult title to find and even first editions can be acquired for quite a modest sum. The Chivers edition is the rarest but should not be too expensive. H&S and CBC editions have a Kiddell Monroe picture of a horse and hay cart on the front board.

At the end of the book the children perform a minstrel show, featuring Rastus and Bones. Some of the words uses reflect their time, but would be unacceptable today. Interestingly, the Armada edition was edited, to omit the words, but the Chivers edition, also 1970, was not.

HODDER & STOUGHTON Hardback 1951 – 1956			
First Edition 1951 (November)			NE1
Boards	Red	Block	Black
Pages	192	Cover price	8/6
ISBN	N/A	Size	19 x 14 cm
Abridged	No	Dustjacket	Joan Kiddell Monroe
Illustrations	12 b/w	Map	Yes (2) (A Spark)
Illustrator	Joan Kiddell Monroe		
Second Impression 1952			
Boards	Green		
Third Impression 1956			
Cover price	9/6		

CHILDREN'S BOOK CLUB Hardback 1952 `NE2`

Boards	Green	Block	Black
Pages	192	Cover price	(3/6)
ISBN	N/A	Size	19 x 12.5 cm
Abridged	No	Dustjacket	Not credited
Illustrations	12 b/w	Map	No
Illustrator	Joan Kiddell Monroe		
Notes	The jacket picture differs from H & S editions and is an adapted colour version of one of the text illustrations.		

BROCKHAMPTON PRESS (HAMPTON LIBRARY)
Hardback 1963 `NE3`

Boards	Orange/red	Block	Black (spine)
Pages	184	Cover price	3/6
ISBN	N/A	Size	19 x 12.5 cm
Abridged	No	Dustjacket	Lilian Buchanan
Illustrations	6 b/w	Map	No
Illustrator	Joan Kiddell Monroe		
Notes	The dustjacket is not credited but is by Lilian Buchanan. A variant has laminated boards, same picture but no cover price.		

CEDRIC CHIVERS LTD Hardback 1970
Revised First Edition `NE4`

Boards	Pictorial	Block	N/A
Pages	192	Cover price	N/K
ISBN	N/A	Size	20 x 14 cm
Abridged	No	Dustjacket	Not credited
Illustrations	12 b/w	Map	No
Illustrator	Joan Kiddell Monroe		
Notes	The cover design features a picture that is a simpler version of the Kiddell Monroe illustration for the H&S editions.		

ARMADA Paperback 1970
Revised First Edition `NE5`

Pages	160	Cover price	2/6 (12½p)
Cat No	C308	Size	17.5 x 10.5 cm
Abridged	Yes	Cover	Not credited
Illustrations	4 b/w	Map	No
Illustrator	Joan Kiddell Monroe		
Notes	The text has been re-written to delete inappropriate words.		

CHRISTMAS AT NETTLEFORD

Elizabeth returns home from boarding school for the Christmas holidays, and her brother Charles is injured cycling home from a friend's house. The adventures involve stolen chickens and a missing musical box. The Owlers are threatened by a rival club, the League of the Red Hand, and a 'war' starts up, which ends with a highly satisfactory snowball fight and a peace agreement. Mr Langton is trying to raise money for his church by holding a Christmas market and the Owlers do their bit to help. Whilst the nativity play rehearsals are taking place the vicarage chickens are stolen. The children are cutting holly at Northend farm when they spot the chicken thief. You will need to read the book to find out more!

A good comparison between the tone of the Lone Pine and Nettleford books is that there are heavy duty sheep rustlers in *The Secret of Grey Walls* and a chicken rustler in this book.

The Chivers edition is, perhaps. the rarest of all Malcolm Saville editions. We did not see a copy when compiling this book and the details come from the only person we know who has a copy.

The Kiddel-Monroe illustrations are very stylish

HODDER & STOUGHTON Hardback 1953-1956			
First Edition 1953 (September)			NE6
Boards	Blue	Block	Black (spine)
Pages	192	Cover price	8/6
ISBN	N/A	Size	19 x 14 cm
Abridged	No	Dustjacket	Joan Kiddell Monroe
Illustrations	12 b/w	Map	Yes (2) (A. Sparks)
Illustrator	Joan Kiddell Monroe		
Second Impression 1956			
Cover price	9/6		
Notes	A copy of this book only came to light as we were going to print and it must, therefore, be considered to be scarce.		

CHILDREN'S BOOK CLUB Hardback 1954 — NE7

Boards	Blue	Block	Green (spine)
Pages	192	Cover price	(3/6)
ISBN	N/A	Size	19 x 13.5 cm
Abridged	No	Dustjacket	Not credited
Illustrations	12 b/w	Map	Yes (2) (as H&S)
Illustrator	Joan Kiddell Monroe		

Notes: The jacket picture differs from H & S editions and is an adapted colour version of one of the illustrations. As in the H&S edition, the maps are simply initialled 'AS'. We have assumed that this is the same A Sparks who is credited in All Summer Through.

BROCKHAMPTON PRESS (HAMPTON LIBRARY) Hardback 1965 — NE8

Boards	Light blue	Block	Green (spine)
Pages	184	Cover price	3/6
ISBN	N/A	Size	18.5 x 12.5 cm
Abridged	No	Dustjacket	Not credited
Illustrations	5 b/w	Map	No
Illustrator	Joan Kiddell Monroe		

ARMADA Paperback 1970
Revised First Edition — NE9

Pages	160	Cover price	3/6 (17½p)
Cat No	C365	Size	17.5 x 11cm
Abridged	Yes	Cover	Not credited
Illustrations	4 b/w	Map	No
Illustrator	Joan Kiddell Monroe		

CEDRIC CHIVERS LTD Hardback 1971
Revised First Edition — NE10

Boards	Pictorial	Block	N/A
Pages	184	Cover price	N/K
ISBN	N/A	Size	18.5 x 12.5 cm
Abridged	No	Dustjacket	Not credited
Illustrations	5 b/w	Map	No
Illustrator	Joan Kiddell Monroe		

Notes: The rarity of this book is very surprising since it was the second Nettleford book from Chivers and the first is seen fairly often. Could it have been withdrawn shortly after publication?

SPRING COMES TO NETTLEFORD

Jimmy takes the lead role in this story. With Paul a victim of whooping cough, Jimmy takes his new bicycle on a train (the Nicky Line) to Smerlsdown. A new character, Margaret Hampton, is duly rescued when she has an accident and she introduces him to a 'secret land' in the woods. Later the children's friend, Mr Wilkins, lends the children an old caravan and their adventures revolve around protecting the nest of some peregrine falcons from egg stealers. The stealing of wild bird eggs was an issue of discussion and legislation in the 1950s and Malcolm Saville clearly makes his own point of view known. The story also involves a point-to-point race and this story epitomises the whole series, with the country children enjoying country pursuits, with just a modicum of danger (in this case a kidnapping) along the way.

Both the Brockhampton and Armada editions omit the last chapter and add an extra paragraph to finish the book.

HODDER & STOUGHTON Hardback 1954
First Edition 1954 (September) — NE11

Boards	Green	Block	Black (spine)
Pages	191	Cover price	8/6
ISBN	N/A	Size	19 x 14 cm
Abridged	No	Dustjacket	Joan Kiddell Monroe
Illustrations	12 b/w	Map	Yes (2)
Illustrator	Joan Kiddell Monroe		

CHILDREN'S BOOK CLUB Hardback — NE12

Boards	Yellow	Block	Black (spine)
Pages	191	Cover price	(3/6)
ISBN	N/A	Size	20 x 13 cm
Abridged	No	Dustjacket	Not credited
Illustrations	12 b/w	Map	Yes (2) (as H&S)
Illustrator	Joan Kiddell Monroe		
Notes	The jacket illustration is not adapted from a text illustration.		

BROCKHAMPTON PRESS (HAMPTON LIBRARY)
Hardback 1964

Boards	Light blue	Block	Black (spine)
Pages	184	Cover price	3/6
ISBN	N/A	Size	18.5 x 12 cm
Abridged	Yes	Dustjacket	Not credited
Illustrations	11 b/w	Map	No
Illustrator	Joan Kiddell Monroe		

ARMADA Paperback 1970
Revised First Edition

Pages	159	Cover price	3/6 (17½p)
Cat No	C403	Size	17.5 x 11 cm
Abridged	Yes	Cover	Not credited
Illustrations	10 b/w	Map	No
Illustrator	Joan Kiddell Monroe		

Introducing the important new novel for Boys and Girls

SPRING COMES TO
NETTLEFORD
by
MALCOLM SAVILLE

Uniform with the
previous ' Nettleford' books
ALL SUMMER THROUGH
and
CHRISTMAS AT NETTLEFORD

each
8/6
net

published
by
HODDER
and
STOUGHTON
London, E.C.4

What the papers said – Nettleford series

'Never dull because of Mr Saville's skill in story writing' Sunday Times (AST)

'Adventures that could happen to anyone' Sheffield Star' (AST)

'Gripping, ably-written, delicately sentimental and entirely wholesome' Junior Bookshelf (CAN)

'Super class' The Scotsman (CAN)

'Will not fail to charm most girls' Shepton Mallet Journal (CAN)

'It's Arthur Ransome country' Time and Tide (SCTN)

'Carefully painted and highly entertaining tale' Church Times (SCTN)

'Ordinary pleasant tale' Times Literary Supplement (SCTN)

'Evokes adventure in the youthful imagination and nostalgia in the mature' Hereford Daily Post (SCTN)

'The author has a strong gift for narrative' Yorkshire Post (TSOBS)

'A really grand adventure' London Evening News (TSOBS)

THE SECRET OF BUZZARD SCAR

In the final book there are some changes. Jimmy does not share in the adventures, which are all set in Yorkshire, where the Langtons have arranged a parish swap/holiday in Swaledale and invited the Richardsons to come along. Mr Richardson, who is not well, sets up some clues to follow and this leads them to old lead mines, ruined houses, waterfalls, caves and adventure. The story features a villain (Ginger Whiskers), rescues, a lot of water and even some love interest. It is certainly the nearest that The Owlers get to being Lone Piners.

The book was published in only three versions but is easy to find. The Children's Book Club edition has the original jacket illustration which is unusual for any CBC title.

HODDER & STOUGHTON Hardback 1955-1956				NE15
First Edition 1955 (October)				
Boards	Green	Block	Black (spine)	
Pages	190	Cover price	8/6	
ISBN	N/A	Size	19.5 x 14	
Abridged	No	Dustjacket	Joan Kiddell Monroe	
Illustrations	8 b/w	Map	Yes (2)	
Illustrator	Joan Kiddell Monroe			
Second Edition 1956				
Cover price	9/6			

CHILDREN'S BOOK CLUB Hardback 1956			NE16	
Boards	Light blue	Block	Black (spine)	
Pages	190	Cover price	(3/6)	
ISBN	N/A	Size	19 x 14 cm	
Abridged	No	Dustjacket	Joan Kiddell Monroe	
Illustrations	8 b/w	Map	Yes (2) (as H&S)	
Illustrator	Joan Kiddell Monroe			
Notes	The dustjacket illustration is the same as H & S editions and the front cover is identical except the colour of the lettering.			

ARMADA Paperback 1972				NE17
Revised 1st Edition				
Pages	158	Cover price	20p	
Cat No	C509	Size	17.5 x 11 cm	
Abridged	Yes	Cover	Not credited	
Illustrations	No	Map	No	

The Secret of Buzzard Scar was also published as a serial in The Children's Newspaper in 1955. Here is part of Malcolm Saville's introduction to episode one plus three of the unique and uncredited illustrations.

"The editor has allowed me to introduce you to a new story about the children of Nettleford. Those of you who have read any of the first three books about the Nettleford Owlers will already, I hope, have made friends with Sally and Paul Richardson, Elizabeth Langton and Jimmy Brand. Jimmy does not appear in this story but the others go north to a part of the country that you can explore for yourself. The only places which are not real in The Secret of Buzzard Scar are Nettleford itself and the village of East Gill.

There are plenty of old mine workings in the fells and there really is a Swinnergill Kirk and a cave behind the waterfall, although when I was there last I could not find the inner cavern. Perhaps you will be luckier!"

They listened to Mr. Richardson entranced

Paul peered down the hole while Keith held his ankles

The beam of Keith's torch stabbed into the darkness

THE SUSAN AND BILL SERIES
PUBLISHED 1954-1961

Although most Malcolm Saville fans love the Lone Pine stories, other series have their advocates too, but not so Susan and Bill. Hardly anyone we know has ever read them. So what can we say to encourage you to consider them? Well, the illustrations for the first six books are by Ernest (Winnie the Pooh) Shepard and are excellent. He is the most famous Saville illustrator. Then, for the collector, there are two complete sets of uniform books - or three, if you include the Portuguese paperbacks, the only Saville books in that language.

Nine year old Susan Brooks and eleven year old Bill Starbright live on a housing estate in the Midlands. Their home and many of the places they visit have not been matched to real locations. However, it is becoming clear that Guildford, where Malcolm Saville was living when he began the series, is a major inspiration. A good example is One Tree Hill, which is just round the corner from his home at Toft House. Saville and Shepard were friends and it is easy to imagine them tramping round the local countryside looking for sites that would feature in both the story and the illustrations.

Malcolm Saville said that he "wrote these stories for younger children because I felt there were not enough tales about children who were going to live for the first time, in new towns and estates on the edge of the country." He wanted children to feel that Susan and Bill were just like them.

Very unusually, the first six books were published in pairs over a three year period. We have put them in, what we think is, the logical order but this is open to argument. Two more books were commissioned but were not written.

SUSAN, BILL AND THE WOLF- DOG

Susan Brooks and her family live in the centre of a smoky Midlands town, but move to a house on a new estate called One Tree Hill. It has been built on the outskirts of town in the grounds of an old manor house, once owned by the crotchety Colonel Whyte. She meets Bill Starbright, who lives next door, and they explore the Colonel's wood, looking for wild animals - they find one too: the colonel's dog Rex. In a heart-warming story, the children and the Colonel come to understand each other better and find out that it is not only Rex whose bark is worse than his bite.

NELSON Hardback 1954-1958
First Edition 1954 — SB1

Boards	Red	Block	Black
Pages	117	Cover price	3/6
ISBN	N/A	Size	18 x 12 cm
Abridged	No	Dustjacket	Ernest Shepard
Illustrations	6 b/w, 1 colour	Map	No
Illustrator	Ernest Shepard		

Second Edition 1954
Third Edition 1958

Cover price	5/-

KNIGHT (BROCKHAMPTON) Paperback 1967-1974
New First Edition 1967 — SB2

Pages	126	Cover price	3/6
ISBN	340 04022 X	Size	17.5 x 11 cm
Abridged	Revised	Cover	'Wayer'
Illustrations	15 b/w	Map	No
Illustrator	Lilian Buchanan		
Notes	A few text alterations with an explanation by Malcolm Saville.		

Revised Second Impression 1974 (January) — SB3

Cover price	25p	Cover	Barry Raynor

Revised Third Impression 1975

Cover price	30p

WHITE LION Hardback 1976
New First Edition 1976 (April)

Boards	Brown	Block	Gilt (spine)
Pages	126	Cover price	£2.50
ISBN	85686 109 X	Size	20 x 13 cm
Abridged	Revised	Dustjacket	Not credited
Illustrations	15 b/w	Map	No
Illustrator	Lilian Buchanan		

What the papers said – Susan and Bill series

'I liked this story very much except for a few places' The Times (Ruth Robbins Age 9) (WD)

'Charm and matter-of-factness' Catholic Herald (WD & ICO)

'When that excellent writer of children's stories, Malcolm Saville, enlists the services as illustrator of that superb draughtsman, Ernest Shepard, the result is a book which should satisfy the most exacting of young critics' Surrey Advertiser (WD & ICO)

'Two delightful books' East Anglian Times (VB & GC))

'Thrilling Experiences' Aberdeen Press (VB & GC)

'Not to be missed' Surrey Advertiser (SK & DS)

'Makes one feel that he is, perhaps, happier when writing for rather older children' Times Literary Supplement (SK &DS))

'Ideal story for a girl aged between seven and twelve'

Northern Evening Telegraph (BSC)

'The holiday makers at Sandy Bay are very unpleasant' East London Advertiser (PB)

'Fans of this writer will know what to expect' Catholic Herald (PB)

SUSAN, BILL AND THE IVY-CLAD OAK

Unusually, it is not until book two of the series that Susan, Bill and their friends form a secret club; this time it is called the Ivy Leaf Club. Of course, there is a rival club and a truculent cousin and much of the book is taken up with recruitment. The story culminates with high drama at Colonel Whyte's cricket match where everyone decides which side they are on.

NELSON Hardback 1954-1958
First Edition 1954
SB5

Boards	Red	Block	Black
Pages	115	Cover price	3/6
ISBN	N/A	Size	18 x 12 cm
Abridged	No	Dustjacket	Ernest Shepard
Illustrations	6 b/w, 1 colour	Map	No
Illustrator	Ernest Shepard		

Second Edition 1954
Third Edition 1958

Cover price	6/-		

WHITE LION Hardback 1975
New First Edition 1975 (January)
SB6

Boards	Red	Block	Gilt (spine)
Pages	115	Cover price	£1.40
ISBN	0 85686 090 5	Size	20 x 13 cm
Abridged	No	Dustjacket	Not credited
Illustrations	7 b/w	Map	No
Illustrator	Ernest Shepard		

KNIGHT (BROCKHAMPTON) Paperback 1976
New First Edition 1976
SB7

Pages	125	Cover price	45p
ISBN	0 340 20501 6	Size	17.5 x 11 cm
Abridged	No	Cover	Barry Raynor
Illustrations	No	Map	No

SUSAN, BILL AND THE VANISHING BOY

The story takes Susan and Bill away from One Tree Hill for the first time, when their parents arrange for them to go on holiday together to a village in Sussex, where they are staying in an old railway carriage at Churtfield station. A boy goes missing and, when Susan sees a face looking out of the other supposedly empty carriage and they find that someone has been living there, the children are not slow to put two and two together. In a thrilling adventure, that involves gypsies and a fun fair, they make some new friends. We will not tell you who one of them is but there is a clue in the title of the book!

NELSON Hardback 1955-1960

First Edition 1955 (March) — SB8

Boards	Red	Block	Black
Pages	120	Cover price	3/6 (later 4/-)
ISBN	N/A	Size	18 x 12 cm
Abridged	No	Dustjacket	Ernest Shepard
Illustrations	6 b/w, 1 colour	Map	No
Illustrator	Ernest Shepard		

Second Edition 1960

Cover price	6/-

KNIGHT (BROCKHAMPTON) Paperback 1968-1975

New First Edition 1968 — SB9

Pages	127	Cover price	3/6
ISBN	340 04023 8	Size	17.5 x 11 cm
Abridged	Revised	Cover	'Wayer'
Illustrations	18 b/w	Map	No
Illustrator	Lilian Buchanan		

Revised Second Edition 1974 (January) — SB10

Cover price	25p	Cover	Barry Raynor

Revised Third Edition 1975

Cover price	30p

WHITE LION Hardback 1977

New First Edition 1977 — SB11

Boards	Green	Block	Gilt (spine)
Pages	120	Cover price	£2.95
ISBN	85686 104 9	Size	20 x 13 cm
Abridged	No	Dustjacket	Not credited
Illustrations	6 b/w	Map	No
Illustrator	Ernest Shepard		

Two famous names

Ernest Howard (E. H.) Shepard (1879 – 1976), who illustrated the first six Susan and Bill books, will always be known for drawing Winnie the Pooh but, in a career that lasted seventy years, his illustrations adorned many books including, famously, Kenneth Grahame's *The Wind in the Willows*. For nearly forty years he contributed cartoons to Punch. He was awarded The Military Cross in 1918, during the Great War; he had worked for British Intelligence, sketching combat areas.

During the 1950s, he lived very close to Malcolm Saville's home in Guildford and one can imagine the idea of the collaboration being discussed over a walk with the dogs or a pint at the local.

Eileen H (Hilda) Colwell (1904 – 2002), to whom all the Susan and Bill books are dedicated, was a librarian, author and storyteller who, almost single-handedly, established the idea of children's libraries in the UK; she was Children's Librarian in Hendon for forty years. She was passionate about children's books and was involved from the start with the Carnegie Medal, the Kate Greenaway Medal, the International Hans Christian Andersen Medal and the Eleanor Farjeon Award (she was a great friend of Farjeon). As a storyteller, she appeared many times on radio and television, most notably on *Play School* and *Jackanory*. She was awarded the MBE in 1965.

She was respected and feared by children's authors, Enid Blyton called her "that woman" and, though Malcolm Saville dedicated these eight books to her, he does not get a mention in her autobiography.

SUSAN, BILL AND THE GOLDEN CLOCK

Malcolm Saville keeps the children down in Sussex, but now they are staying on the farm owned by the family of their friend, John Fraser. A stranger comes to stay at the farm, someone the children have previously seen at a ruined castle. Why is she so interested in Mrs Fraser's clock? A ruined castle, a secret passage, a secret room? If this was Enid Blyton, there would be hidden treasure too, but this is Malcolm Saville.

NELSON Hardback 1955-1960			
First Edition 1955 (March)			SB12
Boards	Red	Block	Black
Pages	118	Cover price	3/6
ISBN	N/A	Size	18 x 12 cm
Abridged	No	Dustjacket	Ernest Shepard
Illustrations	6 b/w, 1 colour	Map	No
Illustrator	E.H. Shepard		
Reprint 1960			
Cover price	6/-		

WHITE LION Hardback 1974			
New First Edition 1974 (April)			SB13
Boards	Yellow	Block	Gilt (spine)
Pages	118	Cover price	£1.40
ISBN	8.5686 033 6	Size	20 x 13 cm
Abridged	No	Dustjacket	Not credited
Illustrations	7 b/w	Map	No
Illustrator	Ernest Shepard		

KNIGHT (BROCKHAMPTON) Paperback 1976			
New First Edition 1976			SB14
Pages	127	Cover price	45p
ISBN	0 340 20500 8	Size	17 x 11 cm
Abridged	No	Cover	Barry Raynor
Illustrations	No	Map	No

SUSAN, BILL AND THE DARK STRANGER

Back home again Susan and Bill go Christmas shopping at a market. They see a small boy, Francis Derwent, running away from an older child. He falls and drops a box containing a games set and the children find out that he had been hoping to sell the games. They are in a café when a man comes in and offers Francis £1 for the box - a lot of money in 1956. Needless to say, the box is worth more than that and, in a surprise ending we find out why. With no paperback edition, you might expect this book to be scarce, but it looks as if both hardback editions were printed in large numbers.

NELSON Hardback 1956-1960
First Edition 1956 (May) — SB15

Boards	Red	Block	Black
Pages	119	Cover price	4/-
ISBN	N/A	Size	18 x 12 cm
Abridged	No	Dustjacket	Ernest Shepard
Illustrations	6 b/w, 1 colour	Map	No
Illustrator	Ernest Shepard		

Reprint 1956
Reprint 1960

Cover price	6/-

WHITE LION Hardback 1973
New First Edition 1973 (May) — SB16

Boards	Blue	Block	Gilt (spine)
Pages	119	Cover price	£1.25
ISBN	8.5686 032 8	Size	20 x 13 cm
Abridged	No	Dustjacket	Not credited
Illustrations	6 b/w	Map	No
Illustrator	Ernest Shepard		
Notes	The book lists all the illustrations as in the Nelson editions but, in fact, the frontispiece is not there.		

SUSAN, BILL AND THE SAUCY KATE

Susan and Bill have had whooping cough and are sent to stay with Bill's Aunt Em at Sandy Bay, on the South Coast. However, after a long journey, she is not there to meet them off the coach, so they go to the beach, where they find an injured dog, stuck in a cave. He belongs to Aunt Em's guest, Miss Pelliford, who is convinced that someone has stolen her dog, Fritz, and ill-treated him on purpose. When they return to the cave, Susan and Bill meet Brenda Thomas, a girl who lives in Sandy Bay, and she offers to take them out on her boat, the Saucy Kate. Later in the story the children become heroes, when Miss Pelliford finds herself in serious trouble.

From this point in the series the Nelson editions tend to be more expensive, though White Lions are still plentiful.

NELSON Hardback 1956-1960			
First Edition 1956 (May)			SB17
Boards	Red	Block	Black
Pages	120	Cover price	4/-
ISBN	N/A	Size	18 x 12 cm
Abridged	No	Dustjacket	Ernest Shepard
Illustrations	6 b/w, 1 colour	Map	No
Illustrator	Ernest Shepard		
Reprint 1960			
Cover price	6/-		

WHITE LION Hardback 1976			
New First Edition 1976 (August)			SB18
Boards	Grey	Block	Gilt (spine)
Pages	120	Cover price	£2.50
ISBN	85686 114 6	Size	20 x 13 cm
Abridged	No	Dustjacket	Not credited
Illustrations	7 b/w	Map	No
Illustrator	Ernest Shepard		

SUSAN, BILL AND THE BRIGHT STAR CIRCUS

Unique in the Malcolm Saville books, the children change the name of their secret club. So it is goodbye to The Ivy Leaf Club and hello to The Bright Star Club, whose aim is to help people in secret. Once again, there is a missing boy and a missing dog but this time there is also a circus theme. The children both visit one and try to set up one of their own. The blurb on the inside flap of the book says that this is their most exciting adventure yet and who are we to disagree with the publicists at Nelson?

For the last two books of the series, Terence Freeman took over as illustrator. He clearly tried to keep to the spirit of Ernest Shepard's originals. Freeman was a prolific illustrator, especially of children's books and, as Terry Freeman, he was also illustrating Lone Pine books at this time. Oddly, for this book only, all the illustrations have a blank page on their reverse.

NELSON Hardback 1960			
First Edition 1960 (June)			SB19
Boards	Red	Block	Black
Pages	121	Cover price	5/-
ISBN	N/A	Size	18 x 12 cm
Abridged	No	Dustjacket	T.R. Freeman
Illustrations	7 b/w, 1 colour	Map	No
Illustrator	T.R. Freeman		

WHITE LION Hardback 1973			
New First Edition 1973 (December)			SB20
Boards	Blue	Block	Gilt (spine)
Pages	121	Cover price	£1.25
ISBN	8 5686 034 4	Size	20 x 13 cm
Abridged	No	Dustjacket	Not credited
Illustrations	8 b/w	Map	No
Illustrator	T.R. Freeman		

SUSAN, BILL AND THE PIRATES BOLD

After seven years and eight books, Susan and Bill make their final bow. It would not be Susan and Bill if they do not make some new friends but they also meet some old friends, including The Saucy Kate, in a return visit to Sandy Bay.

The rector is organising a fundraising carnival and the children get involved. One of their ideas is to dress up as pirates and give rides on the Saucy Kate to an island in the bay. Incidents range from the fairly mundane (shell collecting), to ultra-exciting (rescuing a drowning boy). Even the Rector turns hero as he rescues the children, who are locked in a tower: a rousing finale to a jolly series of books.

We had a look at a well known internet book site and there were over 2000 Susan and Bill books listed, but not one copy of this title. If you see one, snap it up.

NELSON Hardback 1961
First Edition 1961 (March) — SB21

Boards	Red	Block	Black
Pages	117	Cover price	5/-
ISBN	N/A	Size	18 x 12 cm
Abridged	No	Dustjacket	T.R. Freeman
Illustrations	6 b/w, 1 colour	Map	No
Illustrator	T.R. Freeman		

WHITE LION Hardback 1974
New First Edition 1974 (October) — SB22

Boards	Maroon	Block	Gilt (spine)
Pages	117	Cover price	£1.50
ISBN	8.5686 088 3	Size	20 x 13 cm
Abridged	No	Dustjacket	Not credited
Illustrations	6 b/w	Map	No
Illustrator	T.R. Freeman		

This is Malcolm Saville's shortest series, but there are still a number of things that make it unique. For a start, what do we call it? In his biography of Malcolm Saville, *Beyond the Lone Pine*, Mark O'Hanlon calls it The Brown Family series and it is referred to in this way on the back of one of the Armada paperbacks. Fair enough, except that in the first book the children's surname is Gray, only becoming Brown in the paperback. In that version, the title of the book also changes – from *Four and Twenty Blackbirds* to *The Secret of Galleybird Pit*. Neither of these things happens in any other book.

Malcolm Saville never intentionally created a set of new characters for a 'one-off' book. When he wrote *Four and Twenty Blackbirds* in 1959, he obviously intended writing more about the Gray family for in the introduction he describes it "as the first of a new series of stories". Yet, the next new book did not arrive for twelve years. There are clearly a lot of 'whys' about this series.

Humphrey Mervyn Gray/Brown (Humf) and his sister, Lucinda Jane (Lucy), aged 8 and 12, live with their mother and father at the Four and Twenty Blackbirds café in the fictional town of Malling, which is based on Lewes, in Sussex. Their friends in the town are Mark Simson, the vicar's son, and Peggy and John Hogben, who live at Conway's farm and, in a theme often repeated in Malcolm Saville stories, the two townies are introduced to country ways.

FOUR–AND–TWENTY BLACKBIRDS

Lucy and Humf arrive in Malling to discover they will be living at the Four and Twenty Blackbirds café which their parents have bought. They go exploring on their first day and meet some children including Mark, the vicar's son, who warn them to stay away from Galleybird Pit. In a fast moving story the children track down a sheep-killing dog, get involved in a point-to- point and have tea at the vicarage and all the while in a desperate race to get the café opened on time.

Perhaps we exaggerate the excitement, but it is an enjoyable story with the children learning to adapt to life in the country and, as the reviewer in *The Surrey Times & Weekly Press* said "Coming to the end is like leaving a warm room".

The book has a lovely wraparound cover by Lilian Buchanan, featuring all the characters, as they advertise the opening of the café.

It is not terribly difficult to find this book, but the price can vary considerably, so look out for a bargain copy.

NEWNES Hardback 1959			
First Edition 1959 (March)			**LH1**
Boards	Amber	Block	Black (spine)
Pages	159	Cover price	8/6
ISBN	N/A	Size	19 x 12.5 cm
Abridged	No	Dustjacket	Lilian Buchanan
Illustrations	9 b/w	Map	No
Illustrator	Lilian Buchanan		
Notes	There is a variant with green boards and black block.		

THE SECRET OF GALLEYBIRD PIT

The book had originally been published nine years earlier as *Four – and – Twenty Blackbirds* and we believe the change of name was suggested by Malcolm Saville. There had been several, fairly obscure books with the same name, but the well known short story by Agatha Christie did not appear until 1960. The only other examples of a name change are in the American editions of *Mystery at Witchend* and *The Ambermere Treasure*. We can offer no explanation for the other major change: the Gray family are now called Brown, but there do not appear to be any other alterations to the text.

Possibly, as the original book was published by Newnes, Armada acquired the rights to the book along with the Lone Pine stories.

ARMADA Paperback 1967-1976			
First Edition 1967 (July)			**LH2**
Pages	157	Cover price	2/6
Cat No	C191	Size	18 x 11 cm
Abridged	No	Cover	Not credited
Illustrations	9 b/w	Map	No
Illustrator	Lilian Buchanan		
Notes	The illustrations are wrongly credited to Peter Archer, they are those from Four - and - Twenty Blackbirds, so it seems likely that he was the cover artist.		
Second Impression 1969 (July)			
Second Edition 1971 (June)			**LH3**
Cat No	C421	Cover price	17½ p
ISBN 0 00 690421 1	Size	18 x 11 cm	
Abridged	No	Cover	Not credited
Illustrations	9 b/w	Illustrator	Not credited
Notes	Cover and illustrations different from earlier Armada editions.		
Second Impression of Second Edition 1976			
Cover price	40p		

GOOD DOG DANDY

There had been a real police dog with the similar name of Dante and Malcolm Saville had heard of his exploits. In an unusual piece of research, he spent time with police dog handlers, to see for himself how the dogs were trained, and he brings this knowledge to the story. Later, copies of the book were taken into schools by police liaison officers and offered as prizes.

The story finds the children up against burglars and dog poisoners and they learn more about country life when they go camping in Deadman's Wood. Dandy, the police dog, has already visited Humf's school and you can bet he will play a major part as the plot develops.

This is one of a very few Malcolm Saville books, *Home to Witchend* was another, where the paperback edition preceded the hardback. Neither is difficult to find.

ARMADA Paperback 1971-1976			
First Edition 1971 (May)			LH4
Pages	157	Cover price	17½p
Cat No	C420	Size	18 x 11 cm
Abridged	No	Cover	Not credited
Illustrations	No	Map	No
Second Edition 1976			
ISBN	0 00 6904020 3	Cover price	40p

WHITE LION Hardback 1977			
New First Edition 1977			LH5
Boards	Brown	Block	Gilt (spine)
Pages	157	Cover price	£2.75
ISBN	0 85686 243 6	Size	20 x 13 cm
Abridged	No	Dustjacket	Not credited
Illustrations	No	Map	No

THE ROMAN TREASURE MYSTERY

An old Bible with a hidden message, a haunted house and an old coin found in a stream. Who is the mysterious Miss Green and what is she looking for? The clue is in the title, so we are giving nothing away by telling you this is a story of hidden treasure, but who will find it first - the children or the baddies?

This was Malcolm Saville's last story for younger children. After this he would finish his Buckinghams, Marston Baines and Lone Pine series as his career as a writer gradually wound down. Nonetheless this was as good a story as its predecessors. It was the times that had changed.

Like, its predecessor, this was an 'Armada Original' and this time there was no hardback. It is quite difficult to find.

ARMADA Paperback 1973			
First Edition 1973 (August)			
Pages	159	Cover price	25p
Cat No	C750	Size	18 x 11 cm
ISBN	0 00 690750 4		
Abridged	No	Cover	Not credited
Illustrations	No	Map	Yes

What the papers said – Lucy and Humf series

'Human and endearing' Surrey Times and Weekly Press

'Mr Saville is one of a handful of writers who can hold a child's interest consistently' Sheffield Star

'Simple adventure story related with the painstaking skill of a master craftsman' Education Today (GDD)

'One for the younger children' Walthamstow Gazette (TRTM)

THE PICTURES

The images in this section appear in the same order as the books.

Each book is marked with a code which also appears in the relevant section to enable you to match the picture with its description.

LP	The Lone Pine series	OF	Other fiction
MM	The Michael and Mary series	NF	Non-fiction
JS	The Jillies series	OW	Other writing
BU	The Buckinghams series	FE	Foreign Editions
NE	The Nettleford series	TV	TV, film etc
SB	The Susan and Bill series	FO	Follow-on titles
LH	The Lucy and Humf series	AM	About Malcolm Saville
MB	The Marston Baines series		

The pictures are the best we had available so we apologise if the quality of some of the rarer images is poor. We would be delighted to hear from you if you can supply us with a better image!

Where a book cover has not been available, we have indicated this in the description with the initials SNA (Scan Not Available) - again if you are able to provide us with one, we would be delighted to hear from you via mystery@witchend.com

We hope that between the picture and description you will be able to identify any Malcolm Saville books you may come across, and perhaps bag yourself a bargain.

The Lone Pine Series

LP1

LP2

LP3

LP4

LP5

LP6

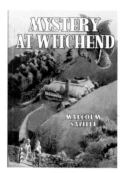

LP7

LP8

LP9

LP10

LP11

LP12

LP13

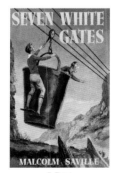

LP14

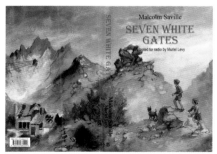

LP15

LP16

LP17

LP18

LP19

LP20

LP22

LP21

LP23

LP24

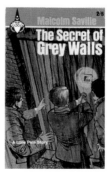

LP25

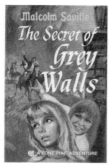

LP26

LP27

LP28

LP29

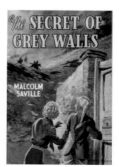

LP30

LP31

LP32

LP33

LP34

LP35

LP36

LP37

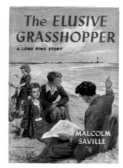

LP38

LP39

LP40

LP41

LP43

LP42

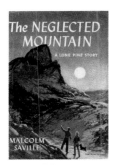

LP44

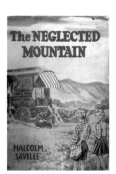

LP45

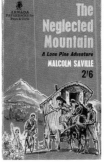

LP46

LP47

LP48

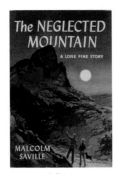

LP49

LP50

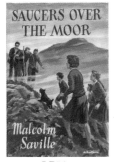

LP51

LP52

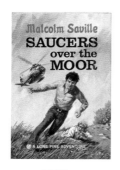

LP53

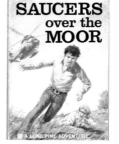

LP54

LP55

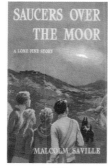

LP56

LP57

LP58

LP59

LP60

LP61

LP62

LP63

LP64

LP66

LP65

LP67

LP68

LP69

LP70

LP71

LP72

LP73

LP74

LP75

LP76

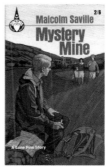

LP77

LP78

LP79

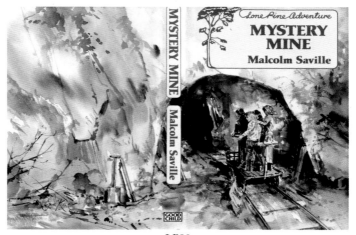

LP80

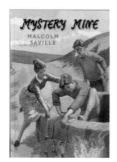

LP81

LP82

LP83

LP84

LP85

LP86

LP87

LP88

LP89

LP90

LP91

LP92

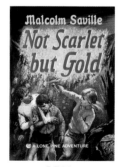

LP93

LP94

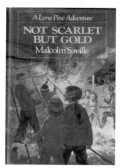

LP95

LP96

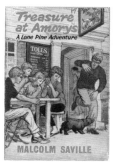

LP97

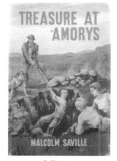

LP98

LP99

LP100

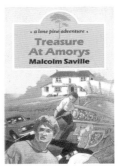

LP101

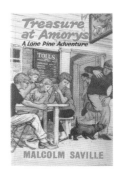

LP102

LP103

LP104

LP105

LP106

LP107

LP108

LP109

LP110

LP111

LP112

LP113

LP114

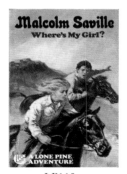

LP115

LP116

LP117

LP118

LP119

LP120

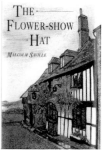

LP121

The Michael and Mary Series

MM1

MM2

MM3

MM4

MM5

MM6

MM7

MM8

MM9

MM10

MM11

MM12

MM13

MM14

MM15

MM16

The Jillies Series

JS1

JS2

JS3

JS4

JS5

JS6

JS7

JS8

JS9

JS10

JS11

JS12

JS13

JS14

JS15

JS16

JS17

JS18

JS19

JS20

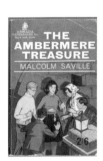

JS21

JS22

JS23

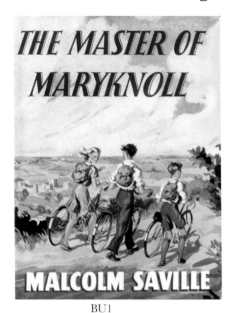

BU1

BU2

BU3

BU4

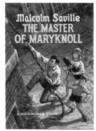

BU6

BU5

BU7

BU8

BU9

BU10

BU11

BU12

BU13

BU14

BU15

BU16

BU17

BU18

BU19

BU20

The Nettleford Series

NE1

NE2

NE3

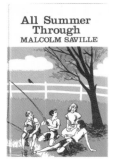

NE4

NE5

NE6

NE7

NE8

NE9

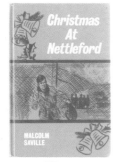

NE10

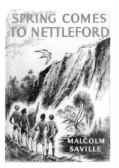

NE11

NE12

NE13

NE14

NE15

NE16

NE17

The Susan and Bill Series

SB1

SB2

SB3

SB4

SB5

SB6

SB7

SB8

SB9

SB10

SB11

SB12

SB13

SB14

SB15

SB16

SB17

SB18

SB19

SB20

SB21

SB22

The Lucy and Humf Series

LH1

LH2

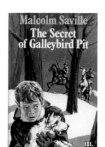

LH3

LH5

LH4

LH6

The Marston Baines Series

MB1

MB2

MB3

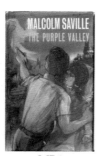

MB4

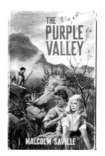

MB5

MB6

MB7

MB8

MB9

MB10

MB11

MB12

MB13

MB14

Other fiction

OF1

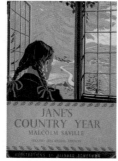

OF2

OF3

OF4

OF5

OF6

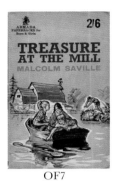

OF7

OF8

OF9

OF10

OF11

OF12

OF13

Non-fiction

NF1

NF2

NF3

NF4

NF5

NF6

NF7

NF8

NF9

NF10

NF11

NF13

NF12

NF14

NF15

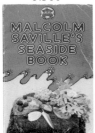

NF16

NF17

NF18

NF19

NF20

NF21

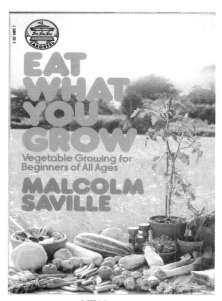

NF22

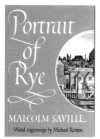

NF23

NF24

NF25

NF26

NF27

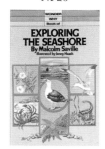

NF28

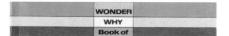

WILD FLOWERS THROUGH THE YEAR

Written by Malcolm Saville Illustrated by Elsie Wrigley

NF29

THE STORY OF
Winchelsea Church

NF30

NF31

NF32

NF33

NF34

NF35

Other writing

OW1

OW2

OW3

OW4

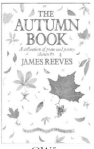

OW5

OW6

OW7

OW8

OW10

CHRISTIAN LIBRARIAN

OW11

OW12

OW13

OW14

OW15

OW16

OW17

176

OW18

OW19

OW20

OW21

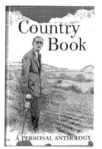

OW23

OW24

OW25

OW26

OW27

OW28

OW29

OW30

OW31

OW32

OW33

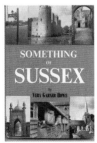

OW34

OW35

OW36

OW37

OW38

OW39

Foreign Editions

FE1

FE2

FE3

FE4

FE5

FE6

FE7

FE8

FE9

FE10

FE11

FE12

FE13

FE14

FE15

FE16

FE17

FE18

FE19

FE20

FE21

FE22

FE23

FE24

FE25

FE26

FE27

FE28

FE29

FE30

FE31

FE32

FE33

FE34

FE35

FE36

FE37

FE38

FE39

FE40

FE41

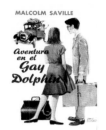

FE42

FE43

FE44

FE45

FE46

FE47

FE48

FE49

FE50

FE51

FE52

FE53

FE54

FE55

FE56

FE57

FE58

FE59

FE60

FE61

FE62

FE63

FE64

FE65

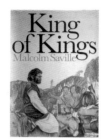

FE66

FE67

FE68

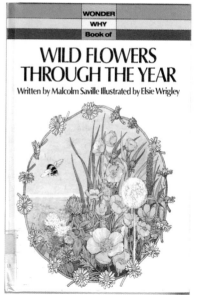

FE69

TV, radio, film and other media
Follow-on titles

TV1

TV2

TV3

FO1

FO2

FO3

About Malcolm Saville

AM1

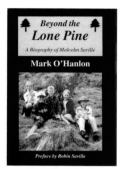

AM2

AM3

AM4

AM5

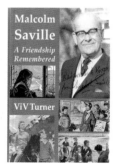

AM6

AM7

THE MALCOLM SAVILLE SOCIETY

The Society was founded in 1994 after a group of enthusiasts enjoyed a trip on a vintage bus to the Shropshire Hills and visited some of the locations featured in the books. Malcolm Saville's son Robin was on that trip and he later asked Mark O'Hanlon and Richard Walker to found a society to celebrate his father's life and work. Over 2,000 members from around the world have joined since 1994.

Mark and Richard set the tone for the Society and it has not changed much since; Malcolm Saville believed strongly in the values of friendship, loyalty, integrity and truth – qualities epitomised in his fictional characters. The Society aims to maintain these values by bringing together those interested to exchange information, discuss the books and to explore the places that inspired his work. Members can enjoy:

Social events

Malcolm Saville set most of his stories in real locations and the Society has organised weekend visits to most of the areas featured. Shropshire and other Lone Pine sites have always been the most popular, but we have been to areas as far apart as Cornwall and Cumbria and also abroad to Amsterdam and Tuscany. Any member is welcome to attend for all or part of a weekend. The Society's annual gathering weekend is held each spring at different locations around the country.

Four Society publications a year

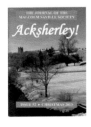

Three times a year members receive a copy of the Society's journal *Acksherley!*, named from an expression often used by the Morton twins in the Lone Pine books. Once a year the Souvenir Programme from the Annual Gathering is sent to all members. You can read more about these publications in the 'About Malcolm Saville' section of this book.

Society lending library

All of Malcolm Saville's books are available for members to borrow in unabridged format for the price of postage.

Independent book search service

Members have access to an independent book search facility which aims to provide them with reasonably priced copies of any books required to complete their collections or if they wish to acquire reading copies.

Application for membership

There is further information on the 'How to Join' section of our website at **www.witchend.com**. The annual cost (at the time of publication) is £15 (UK), £17.50 (Europe) and £21 (Rest of the World). You can join instantly online, using PayPal or BACS payments, or by sending a cheque to the Membership Secretary at Woodside Cottage, 11 Stanford Road, Great Witley, Worcestershire, WR6 6JG.

You can also find us on Facebook at Facebook.com/MalcolmSaville or on Twitter @MSavilleSociety.

THE MARSTON BAINES SERIES
PUBLISHED 1963-1978

The Marston Baines series was written for an older audience than most of Malcolm Saville's books. They are set in a variety of real locations throughout Europe and reflect the changes in the author's own travel patterns. As he grew older he seemed to need the sun on his back a little more. Written during the sixties and seventies the adventures involve topical issues such as drug addiction, satanism and diamond smuggling and seem to reflect his concerns about a world which was rapidly changing and not for the better.

Marston Baines himself is a British secret agent. Aged between 45-50 in the first book, his cover is as an author of thrillers who lives in a cottage on the Sussex Downs. He drives a Mini Cooper which, although stylish, means he is no James Bond. However, although he features in all the books, it is often his nephew, Simon, a student reading modern languages at Oxford, and his friends, who play the major roles. Marston Baines' favourite quotation is said to be "The only thing necessary for the triumph of evil, is that good men do nothing", perhaps something which Malcolm Saville himself felt.

British Marston Baines books were only issued in hardback but most are fairly easy to obtain, though they are often in ex-library condition. They are popular with collectors and first editions in decent condition with jackets can be expensive, especially the final book. If you want to read a paperback version, you will need to brush up on your French.

We do not want to give the plot away but something happens in the final story that you will not find in any other Malcolm Saville book. You will have to read Marston Master Spy to find out what it is.

THREE TOWERS IN TUSCANY

Set in Italy, the first book in the series introduces secret agent, Marston Baines and his nephew, Simon. Simon Baines is invited to visit Marston at Villa Rosa in Fiesole, (near Florence) in Tuscany after the death of Simon's father in a car accident. On his first night he encounters Rosina Conway who has run away from Dr Salvatore, an acquaintance of her parents, with whom she is staying to practise her Italian. Simon's friends from Oxford, Charles Hand and Patrick Cartwright, arrive in the area on holiday and when one of Dr. Salvatore's visitors is murdered, and Rosina disappears, they help Simon to solve the mystery of Dr. Salvatore's activities in the house with three towers.

The book was well received and saw a real departure for Malcolm Saville as he tried to reach an older teenage market. The jacket of the second impression of the book is a real oddity with its green and yellow version of the original full colour artwork.

HEINEMANN – Hardback 1963-1972			
First Edition 1963 (October)			**MB1**
Boards	Blue	Block	Gilt (spine)
Pages	213	Cover price	13/6
ISBN	N/A	Size	20.5 x 13.5 cm
Abridged	No	Dustjacket	Aedwyn Darroll
Illustrations	None	Map	No
Second Impression 1970			**MB2**
Dustjacket	Not credited	Cover price	25/- (£1.25)
ISBN	434 96203 1		
Notes	The artwork is the same as for the first edition but it is printed in shades of green and yellow..		
Third Impression 1972			**MB3**
Boards	Salmon	Cover price	£1.75
Notes	The jacket is not illustrated – there is lettering only and a photo of Malcolm Saville on the rear.		

THE PURPLE VALLEY

Back in Oxford, Simon helps Annabelle Corret when she is nearly run over by a bus. He and Charles then agree to accompany Marston to Provence where Marston had worked with the French resistance during the war. British Intelligence is concerned about imported drugs, which have caused deaths amongst students, and the young people are soon involved in tracking down the drug peddlers and, along the way, have to rescue Marston when he is kidnapped.

Drugs are a constant theme in the Marston Baines books but this is the one in which they are central to the plot. You may find a certain irony in the introduction to the book where Malcolm Saville mentions that British planes dropped cigarettes to the Maquis during the war.

HEINEMANN Hardback 1964-1973				
First Edition 1964 (November)				MB4
Boards	Blue	Block	Gilt (spine)	
Pages	215	Cover price	15/-	
ISBN	N/A	Size	20.5 x 13.5 cm	
Abridged	No	Dustjacket	Not credited	
Illustrations	No	Map	No	
Second Edition 1970				
Boards	Light Blue	Cover price	25/- (£1.25)	
ISBN	434 96202 3			
Third Edition 1973				
Cover price	£1.50			

CHILDRENS BOOK CLUB EDITION Hardback 1965				MB5
Boards	Blue	Block	Black (spine)	
Pages	214	Cover price	(3/6)	
ISBN	N/A	Size	19 x 12.5 cm	
Abridged	No	Dustjacket	Not credited	
Illustrations	No	Map	No	

DARK DANGER

Simon Baines' friend, Patrick Cartwright, is spending his holidays in Venice teaching Count Brindisi's son, Pietro, whose beautiful sister, Francesca is under the influence of an older man, Donelli. Soon he is joined by Simon who is on a mission for his Uncle Marston and they are soon plunged into a story which involves blackmail, a sinister international organisation and the formula for a deadly nerve gas. There are also some scary scenes involving satanists and it is in this area that Malcolm Saville is clearly expressing his concerns in this book.

The second edition has a very plain jacket in a style used for two of the other books. Maybe the publishers were trying to differentiate this series from Malcolm Saville's books for younger readers.

HEINEMANN Hardback 1965-1976

First Edition Oct 1965 — MB6

Boards	Dark grey	Block	Gilt (spine)
Pages	196	Cover price	15/-
ISBN	N/A	Size	20.5 x 13.5 cm
Abridged	No	Dustjacket	Michael Whittlesea
Illustrations	No	Map	No

Second Edition 1976 — MB7

Boards	Blue/green	Block	Silver gilt (spine)
Pages	194	Cover price	£2.60
ISBN	434 96201 5	Dustjacket	Not credited
Notes	No jacket illustration but a photograph of the author on the back.		

CHILDRENS BOOK CLUB EDITION Hardback 1966 — MB8

Boards	Green	Block	Black (spine)
Pages	196	Cover price	(3/6)
ISBN	N/A	Size	19 x 12.5 cm
Abridged	No	Dustjacket	Not credited
Illustrations	No	Map	No

WHITE FIRE

This book is set in Mallorca and, in his introduction, Malcolm Saville talks about the unique nature of Palma. He also anticipates what might happen to the island by mentioning that the Spanish Government is interested in 'selling sunshine'.

Rosina makes a re-appearance in this story, which is about diamond smuggling, and there seems little doubt that she and Simon are becoming a bit more than friends. This is the only story where a child features to any degree: William, the young son of a wealthy industrialist, who is befriended by Rosina but later kidnapped.

As with most of the books in this series, the locations are described in some detail and many of Malcolm Saville's fans feel this is where he is at his best. Although he clearly disapproves of diamond smuggling, this is the first book in the series where he does not seem to have much of an axe to grind.

The book is scarcer than the earlier ones as there is no CBC copy.

HEINEMANN Hardback 1966-1976			
First Edition 1966 (October)			**MB9**
Boards	Brown/tan	Block	Gilt (spine)
Pages	180	Cover price	18/-
ISBN	N/A	Size	20.5 x 13.5 cm
Abridged	No	Dustjacket	Not credited
Illustrations	No	Map	No
Second Edition 1976			**MB10**
Boards	Brick red	Pages	180
Cover price	£2.60	ISBN	434 96204 X
Dustjacket	Not credited		
Notes	The jacket is not illustrated – there is lettering only and a photo of Malcolm Saville on the rear.		

POWER OF THREE

In his introduction, Malcolm Saville calls this a "tale of young love, courage and resource" and this could probably be said of any of the books in the series. This time the danger faced is an evil conspiracy to spread racial hatred and intolerance between people and countries, a subject we can all relate to today.

Annabelle, from *The Purple Valley* is now married to Pierre Radan and living in Brittany and she and her friends, Charles Hand and Kate Boston, who also appeared in that story, feature heavily this time. We meet a sinister triumvirate known as 'The Three' and there is murder along the way. The French police do not cover themselves in glory but the friends do, ably abetted by Marston and Simon.

What do you think of the CBC jacket: ultra stylish or appalling?

HEINEMANN Hardback 1968-1972			MB11
First Edition 1968 (April)			
Boards	Dark blue	Block	Gilt (spine)
Pages	198	Cover price	16/- (later 21/-)
ISBN	434 96205 8	Size	20.5 x 13.5 cm
Abridged	No	Dustjacket	Not credited
Illustrations	No	Map	No
Second Edition 1972			
Boards	Blue	Pages	198
Cover price	£1.60		

CHILDRENS BOOK CLUB EDITION Hardback 1968			MB12
Boards	Green	Block	Black (spine)
Pages	198	Cover price	3/6
ISBN	N/A	Size	19 x 12.5 cm
Abridged	No	Dustjacket	K. Wilson
Illustrations	No	Map	No
Notes	The spine shows the title as The Power of Three		

THE DAGGER AND THE FLAME

Francesca and Patrick make their re-appearance in a story set in the Dolomites where Simon is investigating a secret university which is training students for violent revolution. Malcolm Saville was clearly troubled by student unrest: the riots in Paris were only two years before the book was published, but, unusually, there is no reference to it in his introduction.

HEINEMANN Hardback 1970 – 1975			
First Edition 1970 (June)			MB13
Boards	Red	Block	Gilt (spine)
Pages	156	Cover price	25/- (£1.25)
ISBN	434 96206 6	Size	20.5 x 13.5 cm
Abridged	No	Dustjacket	Ken Sequin
Illustrations	No	Map	No
Second Edition 1975 (June)			
Cover price	£1.90		

What the papers said - Marston Baines series

'Professionally put together' Daily Telegraph (TTIT)

'Priggish young people, unlikely romantic elements but a strong story line' Coventry Evening Telegraph (TPV)

'The Dennis Wheatley of the young' Books and Bookmen (DD)

'The youthful hero and heroine escape murder...but end up in acute danger of marriage' Daily Telegraph (WF)

'Can scarcely fail with future Hammond Innes and Alistair McLean addicts' Children's Book News (POT)

'Opens with a thrill and keeps going' Baptist Times TDATF)

'Lots of excitement and suspense' Evening Argus (MMS)

MARSTON - MASTER SPY

At the end of the 1970s Malcolm Saville brought several of his series to a natural conclusion, notably the Lone Pine series. There is a note at the end of this book which says that it is the last story in the series. You will have to read the book to find out why, but it would have been very difficult for him to have written another one.

In an exciting last bow, Baines is kidnapped from his Sussex home by a secret organisation. Meanwhile the others travel to Luxembourg to investigate the activities of the mysterious Paul Schengen. The story ends with love in the air and decisions which have to be made.

As the book was only published in a single edition, it is quite rare in any condition and will usually be very expensive.

HEINEMANN Hardback 1978			
First Edition 1978 (May)			MB14
Boards	Grey	Block	Gilt (spine)
Pages	145	Cover price	£3.50
ISBN	434 96207 4	Size	20.5 x 13.5 cm
Abridged	No	Dustjacket	Not credited
Illustrations	No	Map	No

Marston Baines

Pierre Radan

Charles Hand

Rosina Conway

Kate Boston

Simon Baines

Annabelle Corot

JANE'S COUNTRY YEAR

This was Malcolm Saville's favourite of all his books (he says so in one of his 1979 newsletters). We also know *Words for All Seasons* was a labour of love for Malcolm Saville and he included two extracts from Jane's Country Year in it. An extract was also included in the anthology *Best Children's Stories of the Year II*.

This is the story of Jane who has been very ill and is sent to stay with her aunt and uncle on a farm in the country for a year. The book is a month-by-month account of what she does and sees throughout the year. Moor End Farm in the book is based on Westend Farm in Wheathampstead, Hertfordshire where Malcolm Saville lived for a number of years. It is still possible to see the similarities in chapter illustrations and the maps, though the latter have the real locations in the wrong places. Will Dickinson, who now runs Westend Farm, has made a study of the book and can clearly identify the locations on the farm.

The book is dedicated to 'Jane Norris (The Jane I know)'. During the research for this book we met Jane Norris and she told us that her father was one of Malcolm Saville's closest friends. Jane did suffer a severe illness as a child and did have to convalesce, but not on a farm and certainly not for a year.

NEWNES Hardback 1946-1953			
First Edition 1946 (November)			OF1
Boards	Brown	Block	Cream
Pages	192	Cover price	12/6
ISBN	N/A	Size	24.5 x 19 cm
Abridged	No	Dustjacket	Bernard Bowerman
Illustrations	32 with spot colour	Map	Yes (2)
Illustrator	Bernard Bowerman		

Second Enlarged Edition 1947 (December)

Boards	Green	Block	Gilt
Pages	224	Cover price	15/-
ISBN	N/A	Size	25 x 19 cm
Abridged	No (extended)	Illustrations	33 spot colour 100+b/w
Illustrator	Bernard Bowerman		
Notes	Now contains a What Jane Saw section for each month. The jacket has the same illustrations but different lettering. A title page vignette has been added. There is a variant with buff boards and gilt block.		

Third Edition 1953 (September)

Boards	Light blue	Block	Black
Pages	256	Cover price	8/6
Illustrations	Over 100 b/w	Size	18.5 x 12.5 cm
Notes	The jacket features a spot colour version of the original. There is a variant with green boards.		

TRANSWORLD (CAROUSEL) Paperback 1974
Revised 1st Paperback Edition 1974

Pages	287	Cover price	35p
ISBN	0 552 54062 5	Size	19 x 12 cm
Abridged	No	Cover	Not credited
Illustrations	118 b/w	Map	Yes (2) (as Newnes)
Illustrator	B. Bowerman		

SECRET OF THE GORGE

In the south of Shropshire, by the borders of Herefordshire, the river Teme runs unexpectedly into a limestone gorge. This is the scene of an astonishing treasure hunt for the Lone Piners which began when Jenny Harman found the faded pages of part of an undated letter in an old horse-hair sofa which her father bought at an auction sale. It is an unfinished letter, and the final words—*where the water*—on the last page, provides their only clue.   10s. 6d. net.

Also by Malcolm Saville . . .

JANE'S COUNTRY YEAR

Not all of us can have the good fortune which came to Jane of spending a whole year in the country on a farm, but we can all share the happy days and months she spent there in Malcolm Saville's delightful account of them.

Boys and girls, and many fathers and mothers, will find *Jane's Country Year* a book of perennial delight—not just to be read and put on the shelf, but a book to which to return from time to time for a smell of the earth and the joys of field and copse, meadow and stream.   8s. 6d.

JOHN AND JENNIFER AT THE FARM

You think you know every book written by an author and then one day someone searches the British Library records under Malcolm Saville's pseudonym: D. J. Desmond and up pops a new book. That is how this book was discovered a few years ago.

This is a book for younger children in the John and Jennifer series, illustrated with photographs by Gee Denes. It is a very simple story with Jennifer going to stay at Sunnylands farm with John and his sisters following her bout of measles. She gets involved in all the farm activities over a period of three months.

This is one of a long series of books featuring John and Jennifer. They were primarily books of photographs, with the text seeming less important, and appeared under the name of the photographer Gee Denes. A number of writers contributed words to the series but this was Malcolm Saville's only effort and it is a matter of conjecture why he used his pseudonym (D. J. Desmond) here.

When this book was listed as by Gee Denes, it sold for a few pounds. Now the text is known to be by Malcolm Saville, it has been seen at several hundred. Such is life!

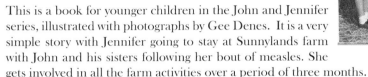

NELSON Hardback 1948 - 1955			
First Edition 1948			OF5
Boards	Green and white	Block	Red
Pages	39	Cover price	7/6
ISBN	N/A	Size	23½ x 20 cm
Abridged	No	Dustjacket	Gee Denes
Photographs	29 colour	Map	No
Photographer	Gee Denes		
Notes	The story is by D. J. Desmond (Malcolm Saville's pseudonym).		
Second Edition 1955			

TREASURE AT THE MILL

This book was written for the Children's Film Foundation. They had found the location, which they thought would make a great background for a children's film and they asked Malcolm Saville to write a story on which they could base it. The Pettit children, Merrilyn, Hilary and Young Harry, who feature in the story, really lived at Spring Valley Mill and also starred in the film with their parents. The book is illustrated by Harry Pettit who was a well known wildlife artist. Older readers may well remember *Little Red Squirrel in Playhour Comic*. As well as a map of the location, there is a wonderful drawing of a plan of the mill and its surroundings, which are all Harry Pettit's work.

This is the only Malcolm Saville book to be set in Essex. John Adams' family home at Spring Valley has been sold and he teams up with the children of the new owners to find treasure hidden there in the Civil War from a clue left among his late father's papers.

At the end of the book Malcolm Saville asked his readers if they would like more stories about the Spring Valley children. It would surely have been a popular series and the reason it never came about was maybe because Harry Pettit died aged 45, little more than a year after the film was released, and the family moved away from Spring Valley.

NEWNES Hardback 1957			
First Edition 1957 (February)			OF6
Boards	Amber	Block	Black (spine)
Pages	152	Cover price	8/6
ISBN	N/A	Size	18.5 x 12.5 cm
Abridged	No	Dustjacket	Harry Pettit
Illustrations	13 b/w	Map	Yes plus plan of mill
Illustrator	Harry Pettit		

ARMADA Paperback 1964			
First Paperback Edition 1964 (February)			OF7
Pages	141	Cover price	2/6
Cat No	C74	Size	17.5 x 11 cm
Abridged	No	Cover	Peter Archer
Illustrations	12 b/w	Map	Yes (as Newnes)
Illustrator	Harry Pettit		
Notes		There is a variant cover: title in blue (rather than purple) and Armada's address has changed from Redhill, Surrey to London. Though later, it cannot be accurately dated.	

RICHARD GRIFFITHS Hardback 2006
New Edition 2006 (December)

Boards	Blue	Block	Red (spine)
Pages	159	Cover price	£18.00
ISBN	978 0 9549069 2 4	Size	19 x 12cm
Abridged	No	Dustjacket	Harry Pettit
Illustrations	13 b/w	Map	Yes (as Newnes)
Illustrator	Harry Pettit		
Notes	Biographical details of the film and some stills on the dustjacket.		

Spring Valley Mill - Now

205

SMALL CREATURES

The *"Truth in a Tale"* series was fifteen little nature story books that had been published in the 1940s. Malcolm Saville agreed to re-write volumes two and three but, in the event, only produced this one: volume two, which had originally been written by Kathleen M. Sully. Volume three would have been called *The Stony Stream*.

The FROG has a skin that is smooth and moist

Charles goes on holiday with his father to stay with Mr and Mrs Brown and their daughter, Julia. Charles is given a notebook to write down all the animals he sees, and the book contains descriptions on the many 'small creatures' found in the local woodland, hedgerows and fields, and is beautifully illustrated.

The purple/gilt version seems to be most common and has been treated as the first edition but there seem to be a myriad of versions. Despite this, and though tiny, the book is not terribly common. It is also well produced on art paper. Consequently, it can be expensive.

The full page colour illustrations in the book were also produced as a series of postcards; the most often seen is *The Frog*.

WARD Hardback 1959			
First Hardback Edition 1959 (June)			**OF9**
Boards	Purple	Block	Gilt (spine)
Pages	64	Cover price	2/6
ISBN	N/A	Size	14 x 10 cm
Abridged	No	Dustjacket	John T Kenney
Illustrations	10 colour, 8 b/w	Map	No
Illustrator	John T Kenney /Rene Cloke (one picture from original book)		
Notes	There are a number of variants of this book with different coloured boards/block. We have seen brown/gilt, light blue/gilt, dark blue/gilt and pale green/red. One copy had an increased cover price of 4/-. The most significant variant is one with a laminated cover with the original jacket design but no price or cover flap information.		

THE THIN GREY MAN

This book is set on the South Downs and involves Rose and Jimmy Towner and their dog, Ringo. They become involved in an adventure about the smuggling of watches from France after Rose sees a helicopter in trouble and someone takes the clothes from a scarecrow. It was clearly meant to be the first in new series but remained a 'one-off'.

MACMILLAN Hardback 1966
First Hardback Edition 1966 — OF10

Boards	Illustrated (as jacket)	Block	N/A
Pages	128	Cover price	11/6
ISBN	N/A	Size	19.5 x 13 cm
Abridged	No	Dustjacket	Desmond Knight
Illustrations	18 b/w	Map	No
Illustrator	Desmond Knight		

ABELARD-SCHUMAN (Grasshopper) Hardback 1974
New First Hardback Edition 1974 — OF11

Boards	Lime green	Block	Gilt
Pages	128	Cover price	£1.25
ISBN	0 200 72197 6	Size	20 x 13 cm
Abridged	No	Dustjacket	Desmond Knight
Illustrations	17 b/w	Map	No
Illustrator	Desmond Knight		
Notes	There is a different jacket from the Macmillan edition. Grasshopper editions have amended artwork - 1970s hairstyles.		

ABELARD-SCHUMAN (Grasshopper) Paperback 1974
New First Edition — OF12

Pages	128	Cover price	45p
ISBN	0 200 72198 4	Size	19 x 12 cm
Abridged	No	Cover	Desmond Knight
Illustrations	17 b/w	Map	No
Illustrator	Desmond Knight		

STRANGE STORY

Throughout his life, Malcolm Saville was a practising Christian and Christian themes can be seen in some of his work, though they are not overt. This, however, is an account of the story of Jesus as told by a Roman legionary, Lucius, to two Roman children, Claudia and Marcus.

Though set 2,000 years ago, in the foreword Malcolm Saville still draws our attention to the real locations in the story "perhaps in your lifetime travel by air will be so easy and cheap that you will be able to see what remains of some of the little towns and villages, as well as the actual green hills and snow capped mountains and the lovely lake at Galilee where so many strange words were spoken and surprising things happened".

The book is not very common but is usually inexpensive. This may be because it does not fit into any particular genre. We had to think hard about which section of this book to put it in and plumped for *Other Fiction* as it is written as a novel, but we would not wish to offend anyone by suggesting that the story within the book is fiction. Perhaps the last words should be with Malcolm Saville writing in 1968:

"My book is an attempt to retell the truth to boys and girls who are ignorant of, or virtually untouched by, Christianity – the truth that is yesterday, today and tomorrow."

MOWBRAY Hardback 1967			
First Hardback Edition 1967 (October)			OF13
Boards	Red	Block	Gilt
Pages	132	Cover price	10/6
Cat No	07187	Size	18.5 x 12.5 cm
Abridged	No	Dustjacket	Signed 'Hermsen'
Illustrations	12 b/w	Map	Yes
Illustrator	Unknown		

For an author best known for his children's fiction, Malcolm Saville wrote a large number of non-fiction books throughout his career.

Although we know he researched his stories by visiting the locations and picking up old legends etc, it is still the case that the process is essentially to sit down and let the imagination drive the narrative. With non-fiction, an in-depth knowledge of the subject is required, though a general interest is helpful. Books are usually based on thorough research. So it is worth mentioning again that Malcolm Saville was never a full-time writer. For most of his life he had a full-time and fairly onerous job. After his retirement he would certainly have had more time, but, in fact, the later books did not require the same depth of research as the earlier ones. He was certainly a man with tremendous energy managing to balance his professional and writing careers with a full social and family life. Quite an achievement.

Of course, the information he gleaned in the research for his non- fiction work was not wasted when writing his stories, especially the extensive knowledge which he had of country matters. The countryside with its animals and plants, the seaside and the various parts of England that he visited were integral parts of his fiction.

He might have written a Sussex guide book or started his Shropshire book somewhat earlier. His interest in cricket and football hardly get a mention, but what he has left us is a body of work which tells us about a man with wide- ranging and deep interests and is well worth reading.

AMATEUR ACTING AND
PRODUCING FOR BEGINNERS

This is a notable book as it was Malcolm Saville's first. It was written under the pseudonym of D. J. Desmond, which Malcolm Saville used for two books and some articles during his early writing career. We do not know where this name originated.

Both Malcolm Saville and his wife were active in pre-war amateur dramatics in Harpenden, Hertfordshire and the book suggests he was involved both as an actor and on the production side, though this was a subject that he did not return to.

THE BLANKTOWN PLAYERS present

**The Late
Christopher
Bean**

at the

PUBLIC HALL

BLANKTOWN

MARCH 23rd & 24th at 8.15 p.m.

Cast includes :

JOHN BAILEY   HENRY EVERETT
MARY CAVENDISH   DUDLEY HINE
DORIS DEAN   RUTH JONES

BOOK SEATS NOW at Jones's Library
Reserved, 3/6 and 2/6.   Unreserved, 1/-

Until the later stages of preparing this book we had thought the rather plain orange dustjacket was the only one that existed so it was a surprise to come across the illustrated jacket. We think that this is the first one, the main reason is that it shows a cover price of 2/- whilst the orange cover shows 2/6. The book, however, is identical.

It may be that the book was re-launched, but it is not clear when this happened. The illustrated cover has advertisements for Pearson's *Books for Amateurs* series. These had been in print for some years. The orange cover features their *Beginner* series and these were all recent. The orange jacket often has a price sticker showing 1/9.

The book includes stage diagrams, a suggested playbill and an advertisement for French's play catalogue.

C. ARTHUR PEARSON Hardback 1937			
First Edition 1937			NF 1/2
Boards	Dark Orange	Block	Black
Pages	109	Cover price	2/-
ISBN	N/A	Size	19 x 13 cm
Illustrations	Only plans	Dustjacket	Not credited
Notes	There is a second jacket which is orange with black lettering.		

THE SCRAP-BOOKS

The content and style of this short series of books are fairly typical of many books published in the post-war years where writers would tackle a subject which interested them and include pieces of poetry by other authors to illustrate it. Malcolm Saville would return to both theme and style later in his career and it was a mark of how far he had come in such a short time that he was given the opportunity to write these books in a time of fairly acute paper shortages.

The books were all in a very similar format and were all originally published under the War Economy Standard. They all have a large number of photographs, but only the *Open Air* and *Seaside Scrap-books* have other illustrations. Despite their age, these books are quite easy to find and must have been produced in large numbers.

COUNTRY SCRAP-BOOK FOR BOYS AND GIRLS

The first book concentrates on the flora and fauna of the English countryside and country pursuits, and features poems by Shelley and Browning, among others, and a small prose piece called *The First Storm of Autumn* by D. J. Desmond, Malcolm Saville's pseudonym.

NATIONAL MAGAZINE CO. Hardback 1944			
First Edition 1944 (October)			NF 3
Boards	Red	Block	Gilt
Pages	127	Cover price	5/-
ISBN	N/A	Size	18.5 x 12.5 cm
Illustrations	B/w photographs	Dustjacket	C.F. Tunnicliffe

GRAMOL Hardback 1945-1946			
Second (Enlarged) Edition 1945			NF 4
Pages	144	Cover price	7/6
Notes	Though the publisher appears to have changed, the book is very similar to the original. The major difference is that there is an extra chapter called "Rivers, Ponds & Streams". In the Gramol edition, the cover illustrations are now on a pink background where originally it was predominantly blue. The background material on the dustjacket has also been re-written.		
Third Edition 1946			

OPEN AIR SCRAP-BOOK FOR BOYS AND GIRLS

The second title is on similar themes, but concentrates on living in, and enjoying, the country. It covers favourite Saville areas such as Shropshire, the South Downs and Romney Marsh and gives advice on camping and map reading. Writers include Shakespeare and Wordsworth.

GRAMOL Hardback 1945-1946			
First Edition 1945 (November)			NF 5
Boards	Blue	Block	Gilt
Pages	143	Cover price	7/6
ISBN	N/A	Size	18.5 x 12.5 cm
Illustrations	The Harts	Dustjacket	C.F. Tunnicliffe
Notes	Includes b/w photographs		
Second Impression 1946			

SEASIDE SCRAP-BOOK FOR BOYS AND GIRLS

The final book features coast and seaside themes. Malcolm Saville's introduction recognises that, just after the war, many children may not have seen, or had a holiday by the sea. Poems by Tennyson and Longfellow are included. Once again, his birth county of Sussex gets special mentions and there are chapters about the Coastguard and the Royal National Lifeboat Institution.

GRAMOL Hardback 1946			
First Edition 1946 (September)			NF 6
Boards	Green	Block	Gilt
Pages	144	Cover price	7/6
ISBN	N/A	Size	18.5 x 12.5 cm
Illustrations	The Harts	Dustjacket	C.F. Tunnicliffe
Notes	Includes b/w photographs.		

THE ADVENTURE OF THE LIFE-BOAT SERVICE

In recent years, Malcolm Saville had written a number of articles celebrating various heroes of British life, including one about life-boat men. This book is not very much more than a long article, as its 70 pages are crammed with 58 black and white photographs. The cover illustrator is Claude Muncaster who was well-known, particularly as a marine painter, and had served as a naval reservist during the war. His dramatic picture was used for both the cover and as a frontispiece.

MACDONALD & CO. Hardback 1950 (Dec)			
First Edition 1950 (December)			NF 7
Boards	Red	Block	Black
Pages	80	Cover price	6/-
ISBN	N/A	Size	21 x 16cm
Illustrations	b/w photographs	Dustjacket	Claude Muncaster

THE CORONATION GIFT BOOK
FOR BOYS AND GIRLS

Many books were published for the 1953 Coronation and this must have done well as it went into three impressions. It tells the history of the event and sets the scene for what could be expected when the Queen was crowned. The book is lavishly illustrated with photographs (seven in colour) and drawings. John Harris painted the wraparound cover, but nothing else is credited. One of the photographs is of Malcolm Saville at Westminster Abbey Library.

DAILY GRAPHIC/PITKIN PICTORIALS Hardback 1952-1953			
First Edition 1952 (November			NF 8
Boards	Deep red	Block	Gilt
Pages	80	Cover price	8/6
ISBN	N/A	Size	24.5 x 19 cm
Illustrations	Not credited	Dustjacket	John Harris
Notes	Includes b/w photographs.		
Second Impression 1952 (December)			
Third Impression 1953			
Notes	Now published by Pitkin Pictorials only.		

KING OF KINGS

Malcolm Saville's religious belief was very important to him and this re-telling of the life of Christ was well received when it was originally published. The Lion edition in the 1970s formed the basis of three foreign editions, two virtually identical in format.

The first edition appears with both a rather dull jacket with no illustration and a full colour version showing the Adoration of the Magi. The duller version came first so you should bear this in mind when purchasing. Booksellers may not realise that two versions exist.

KING OF KINGS
The story of our Lord
retold for young people by
MALCOLM SAVILLE

This famous writer's simple, sincere and straightforward narrative
—never shirking the controversial aspects of the Gospel story—
will make its appeal to older readers also. It is a beautiful book to
give or to be given.

2 colour plates, 22 halftones, 4 maps 21s
coming November 13

NELSON Hardback 1958
First Edition 1958 (November) — NF 9/10

Boards	Blue	Block	Gilt (spine)
Pages	264	Cover price	21/-
ISBN	N/A	Size	22 x 14.5 cm
Illustrations	B/w photographs	Dustjacket	Not illustrated
Notes	There is a variant with an illustrated cover (not credited).		

Second Impression 1958 (December)

Cover price	25/-		
Notes	There is a variant with red boards and black block.		

LION PUBLISHING Hardback 1975
Revised Edition 1975 (September) — NF 11

Boards	Brown	Block	Gilt (spine)
Pages	168	Cover price	£2.95
ISBN	0 85648 038 X	Size	22.5 x 16 cm
Illustrations	Kathy Wyatt	Dustjacket	Kathy Wyatt
Notes	The text has been re-written and includes colour photographs.		

LION (ASLAN) Paperback 1978
First Paperback Edition 1978 (November) — NF 12

Pages	168	Cover price	£1.25
ISBN	0 85648 126 2	Size	19.5 x 11.5
Illustrations	Kathy Wyatt	Cover	Not credited
Notes	The text is same as 1975 edition but without photographs.		

'MALCOLM SAVILLE'S' BOOKS

These are similar in theme to the earlier scrap-books and once again were encouraging British children to explore their country. The hardbacks are full of black and white and colour photographs as are the paperbacks, but here there are fewer and they are different. These books are easy to find, but the hardbacks are often ex-library copies.

MALCOLM SAVILLE'S COUNTRY BOOK

CASSELL Hardback 1961			
First Edition 1961 (October)			NF 13
Boards	Blue	Block	Gilt (spine)
Pages	86	Cover price	12/6
ISBN	N/A	Size	21.5 x 14 cm
Illustrations	M McGuinness	Dustjacket	Photograph

CAROUSEL (TRANSWORLD) Paperback 1973			
Revised First Paperback Edition			NF 14
Pages	140	Cover price	30p
ISBN	0 552 54030 7	Size	19 x 12 cm
Illustrations	M McGuinness	Cover	Not credited

MALCOLM SAVILLE'S SEASIDE BOOK

CASSELL Hardback 1962			
First Edition 1961 (October			NF 15
Boards	Blue	Block	Gilt (spine)
Pages	88	Cover price	15/-
ISBN	N/A	Size	21.5 x 14 cm
Illustrations	M. P. McGuinness	Dustjacket	Photograph

CAROUSEL (TRANSWORLD) Paperback 1973			
Revised First Paperback Edition 1974 (May)			NF 16
Pages	126	Cover price	30p
ISBN	0 552 54054 4	Size	19 x 12 cm
Illustrations	M. P. McGuinness	Cover	Not credited
Revised Second Paperback Edition 1975			
Cover price	35p		

THE 'COME TO' BOOKS

After more than 30 years as a writer, Malcolm Saville wrote a series of guide books. He started with London, a city in which he had lived and worked, which he knew well and which featured in some of his stories. After a gap of three years, three more books appeared featuring the three south western counties, but these were for a new publisher and in a different format. They also had simultaneous paperback editions which were virtually identical. It is perhaps surprising that the series was not extended to include the two counties that were most dear to his heart, Shropshire and Sussex, but this may have been a decision made by the publishers.

COME TO LONDON

HEINEMANN Hardback 1967			
First Edition 1967 (April)			NF 17
Boards	Dark blue	Block	Silver (spine)
Pages	150	Cover price	21/-
ISBN	N/A	Size	18.5 x 12.5 cm
Illustrations	Leslie Atkinson	Dustjacket	Photograph
Notes	Contains b/w photographs and maps by Penny Carey as well as a wraparound photographic dustjacket.		

COME TO DEVON

ERNEST BENN LTD Hardback 1969			
First Edition 1969 (April)			NF 18
Boards	Orange/red	Block	Silver (spine)
Pages	128	Cover price	18/-
ISBN	510 17010 2	Size	21.5 x 14 cm
Illustrations	b/w photographs	Dustjacket	Photograph

ERNEST BENN LTD Paperback 1969			
First Paperback Edition 1969 (April)			NF 18
Pages	128	Cover price	7/6
ISBN	510 17011 0	Size	21 x 13.5 cm
Illustrations	B/w photographs	Cover	Photograph

COME TO CORNWALL

ERNEST BENN LTD Hardback 1969
First Edition 1969 (July)

Boards	Dark blue	Block	Silver (spine)
Pages	128	Cover price	18/- (90p)
ISBN	510 17021 7	Size	21.5 x 14 cm
Illustrations	B/w photographs	Dustjacket	Photograph
Notes	The jacket is predominantly blue but a red variant exists, though this is very rare.		

ERNEST BENN LTD Paperback 1969
First Paperback Edition 1969 (July)
NF 19

Pages	128	Cover price	9/- (45p)
ISBN	510 17022 5	Size	21 x 13.5 cm
Illustrations	B/w photographs	Cover	Photograph

COME TO SOMERSET

ERNEST BENN LTD Hardback 1970
First Edition 1970 (March)
NF 20

Boards	Green	Block	Silver (spine)
Pages	128	Cover price	18/- (90p)
ISBN	510 17031 5	Size	21.5 x 14 cm
Illustrations	B/w photographs	Dustjacket	Photograph

ERNEST BENN LTD Paperback 1970
First Paperback Edition 1970 (March)
NF 20

Pages	128	Cover price	10/- (50p)
ISBN	510 17032 3	Size	21 x 13.5 cm
Illustrations	B/w photographs	Cover	Photograph

The three books on the south western counties feature statues of famous local men. They are Sir Francis Drake in Plymouth (Devon), Richard Trevithick in Camborne (Cornwall) and Admiral Blake in Bridgwater (Somerset). *Come to London* has Tower Bridge on the front and the Houses of Parliament on the back.

SEE HOW IT GROWS

This is the only book which Malcolm Saville wrote for the OUP and is an introduction to gardening for children. It includes a month-by-month guide to gardening activities. He was well qualified to write a book like this with both his experience as a children's writer and having worked at *My Garden* magazine for some years after the war. He was also in retirement at this time so may have had more time for his own gardening, although anecdotal evidence suggests he may always have been more of a theoretical gardener than a practical one.

OXFORD UNIVERSITY PRESS Hardback 1971			
First Edition 1971 (September)			NF 21
Boards	Illustrated	Block	N/A
Pages	72	Cover price	£1.25/25/-
ISBN	0 19 273124 6	Size	24.5 x 19 cm
Illustrations	Robert Micklewright	Dustjacket	Robert Micklewright

EAT WHAT YOU GROW

During the last few years of his life, Malcolm Saville had a number of books published by Carousel, mostly in this small paperback format. They were quite short and covered subjects which he knew well. The title of this book is self-explanatory. In the introduction he suggests it is aimed at all beginners, but it was clearly for children. It is an extremely difficult book to get hold of but, oddly, it sometimes turns up in Australia.

CORGI CAROUSEL (TRANSWORLD) Paperback			
First Edition 1975 (June)			NF 22
Pages	96	Cover price	30p
ISBN	0 552 54075 7	Size	19.5 x 12.5 cm
Illustrations	Robert Micklewright	Cover	Robert Micklewright

PORTRAIT OF RYE

By 1976, Malcolm Saville was living in Winchelsea and there are stories of his readers visiting him and being taken to Rye to visit Lone Pine locations. It was a place that was very special to him and had been the backdrop for a number of his books since the 1940s. It must, therefore, have delighted him to write this guidebook. The original book is surprisingly difficult to find, even though it was published simultaneously in paperback and hardback and this encouraged Mark O'Hanlon to re-publish it. The original illustrations were woodcuts by Michael Renton and, although the book is fairly scarce, it often turns up signed by author, illustrator or, if you are lucky, both. The book also contains a poem, simply called *Rye*, by "my friend, the poet, Patric Dickinson".

HENRY GOULDEN Hardback Edition 1976
First Edition 1976 (November) — NF 23

Boards	Tan	Block	Gilt (spine)
Pages	93	Cover price	£5.00
ISBN	0 904822 05 2	Size	22 x 15 cm
Illustrations	Michael Renton	Dustjacket	Michael Renton

HENRY GOULDEN Paperback 1976
First Paperback Edition 1976 (November) — NF 23

Pages	93	Cover price	£3.50
ISBN	0 904822 06 0	Size	21 x 15cm
Illustrations	Michael Renton	Dustjacket	Michael Renton

MARK O'HANLON Paperback
Revised Paperback Edition 1999 — NF 24

Pages	126	Cover price	£8.99
ISBN	0 9528059 2 8	Size	20.5 x 14.5 cm
Cover	John C. Allsup	Illustrations	11 b/w, 1 map
Illustrator	John C. Allsup		
Notes	Revised and updated from 1976 edition.		

THE QUIZ BOOKS

A departure in 1978 was two quiz books from Carousel, re-visiting subjects that he had written about throughout his writing career. Many of the questions are based on Robert Micklewright's drawings and are a mixture of downright easy and pretty difficult. It is interesting to see that, even at this late stage of his career, Malcolm Saville was still encouraging children to write to him and his introductions include his address in Winchelsea, which he says is less than a kilometre from the sea. Surely in earlier days he would have said about half a mile and we can imagine an interesting conversation with the publisher about this.

THE COUNTRYSIDE QUIZ

The book is divided into seasons with an introduction to each and some poems. Do you know another name for the green plover? You might if you have followed the adventures of the Lone Piners.

CORGI CAROUSEL (TRANSWORLD) Paperback 1978-1979			
First Paperback Edition 1978			NF 25
Pages	127	Cover price	60p
ISBN	0 552 54133 8	Size	19.5 x 12.5 cm
Illustrations	Robert Micklewright	Cover	Robert Micklewright
Second Paperback Edition 1979			

THE SEASHORE QUIZ

This time the chapters concern different aspects of the seaside: fish, birds, shells, etc. Do you know which sea bird is sometimes called the sea mew? If not you will have to read the book to find out.

CORGI CAROUSEL (TRANSWORLD) Paperback 1981			
First Paperback Edition 1981 (June)			NF 26
Pages	128	Cover price	75p
ISBN	0 552 54176 1	Size	19.5 x 12.5 cm
Illustrations	Robert Micklewright	Cover	Robert Micklewright

WONDER WHY BOOKS

The Wonder Why series was fairly typical of a genre that has been popular with parents for many years, but perhaps less so with children. This was a series of over 20 books on science and nature subjects. Malcolm Saville must have been an obvious person to ask to contribute and he must have been pleased to get the commission at a time when he was finding it difficult to get his fiction published. His subjects were those that he had been writing about for 30 years. The hardback and paperback editions are virtually identical.

EXPLORING A WOOD

The most surprising thing about this book was that there was a Spanish edition. It is difficult to understand why children in Spain would be interested in exploring a British wood.

CAROUSEL (TRANSWORLD) Hardback 1978
First Edition 1978 (May) — NF 27

Boards	Illustrated	Block	N/A
Pages	32	Cover price	£1.50
ISBN	0 552 98071 4	Size	28 x 21 cm
Illustrations	Elsie Wrigley	Cover	Elsie Wrigley

CAROUSEL (TRANSWORLD) Paperback 1978
First Paperback Edition 1978 (May) — NF 27

Pages	32	Cover price	60p
ISBN	0 552 57026 5	Size	28 x 21 cm
Illustrations	Elsie Wrigley	Cover	Elsie Wrigley

EXPLORING THE SEASHORE

Like the other two books this is profusely illustrated but is the only one where Jenny Heath provided the drawings. None of the Wonder Why books are common, though you might consider buying the virtually identical American edition.

CAROUSEL (TRANSWORLD) Hardback 1979			
First Edition 1979 (May)			NF 28
Boards	Illustrated	Block	N/A
Pages	32	Cover price	£1.50
ISBN	0 552 98089 7	Size	28 x 21 cm
Illustrations	Jenny Heath	Cover	Jenny Heath

CAROUSEL (TRANSWORLD) Paperback 1979			
First Paperback Edition 1979 (May)			NF 28
Pages	32	Cover price	75p
ISBN	0 552 57033 8	Size	28 x 21 cm
Illustrations	Jenny Heath	Cover	Jenny Heath
Second Edition 1979			

WILD FLOWERS THROUGH THE YEAR

Elsie Wrigley was once more the artist for the final book where Malcolm Saville wrote the words. Together with Paul Wrigley she had also illustrated *Words for All Seasons*.

CAROUSEL (TRANSWORLD) Hardback 1980			
First Edition 1980 (September)			NF 29
Boards	Illustrated	Block	N/A
Pages	32	Cover price	£1.50
ISBN	0 552 98117 6	Size	28 x 21 cm
Illustrations	Elsie Wrigley	Cover	Elsie Wrigley

CAROUSEL (TRANSWORLD) Paperback 1980			
First Paperback Edition 1980 (September)			NF 29
Pages	32	Cover price	85p
ISBN	0 552 57041 9	Size	28 x 21 cm
Illustrations	Elsie Wrigley	Cover	Elsie Wrigley

THE STORY OF WINCHELSEA CHURCH

If you go into any church in England over 100 years old you will find a pile of booklets and an invitation to take one but leave a contribution. Winchelsea church, and the small town that surrounds it, have a history that would beat most.

By 1979 Malcolm Saville had retired to Winchelsea and must have been an obvious person to re-write the little booklet about his local church. The original had been written by Gertrude Leigh and we know it had reached it sixth edition by 1929 when it was revised by the Rev R A Cochrane. The 18th to 21st editions included photographs by A. Vaughan Kimber, including a colour centrefold. Although the text is virtually the same in all four, there are variations between the editions on page 10, relating to the giving of donations for the upkeep of the church. In 2004 a full colour version appeared with photographs by Chris Parker and Melvyn Pett and the text was slightly revised by Robert Hargreaves. In 2009 this was updated with a new cover photograph and minor text changes.

PRIVATE PUBLICATION Paperback 1978 – 2004			
18th Paperback Edition			**NF 30**
Pages	36	Cover price	(75p)
ISBN	N/A	Size	19.5 x 12.5 cm
Illustrations	Photographs	Cover	Photograph
19th Paperback Edition 1979			
20th Paperback Edition 1980			
21st Paperback Edition 1980			
22nd Paperback Edition 2004			**NF 31**
Pages	34	Cover price	£2.50
ISBN	N/A	Size	21.5 x 17 cm
Illustrations	Photographs	Cover	Photograph
23rd Paperback Edition 2009			**NF 32**

WORDS FOR ALL SEASONS

In his introduction to this book Malcolm Saville calls it a dream come true. With half a lifetime of his own works behind him, he was given the chance to publish an anthology of his favourite poetry and prose linking the turning of the seasons with his Christian faith. The title is taken from a play on the Robert Whittinton's description of Sir Thomas More as "a man for all seasons". The book includes two short passages from Jane's Country Year and selections from, among others, William Wordsworth, Robert Frost, Rupert Brooke and William Blake. The paperback version of this book is very scarce and any copies seen are well worth snapping up.

The hardback is still available but it is possible that these are the remains of the original print run. The original dustjacket has a yellow background but this was later re-printed with a pink background and with a revised price of £9.95. The book is now sold without a dustjacket and the latest price is £13.25.

LUTTERWORTH PRESS Hardback 1979			
First Edition 1979 (August))			NF 33
Boards	Purple or Green	Block	Gilt (spine)
Pages	192	Cover price	£4.95
ISBN	0 7188 2393 1	Size	21.5 x 14 cm
Illustrations	Elsie & Paul Wrigley	Dustjacket	Elsie & Paul Wrigley

LION Paperback 1981			
First Paperback Edition 1981			NF 34
Pages	192	Cover price	£1.50
ISBN	0 85648 475 X	Size	17.5 x 11
Illustrations	Elsie & Paul Wrigley	Cover	Colour Photographs

THE SILENT HILLS OF SHROPSHIRE

Malcolm Saville was born in Sussex, lived much of his life there and died there too. His family grew up in Hertfordshire and he also lived in London and Surrey. All these places appear in his books, but probably the county he is most associated with is Shropshire. Here was located the Lone Pine and here was Witchend - the house that would feature in so many of the Lone Piners' adventures. Yet, although he would publish guides to Rye, London and the counties of Devon, Cornwall and Somerset, he did not publish a book on Shropshire during his lifetime

He did plan one though and left an unfinished manuscript with an introduction and first chapter already written and a synopsis for the other chapters. Author Mark O'Hanlon and illustrator John Allsup are both Malcolm Saville devotees and had a once in a life-time opportunity to complete the book. Mark has skilfully written the remaining chapters and John's black and white illustrations are sympathetically done.

MARK O'HANLON Paperback			
First Paperback Edition 1998			NF 35
Pages	140	Cover price	£8.99
ISBN	0 9528059 1 X	Size	20.5 X 14.5 cm
Illustrations	John C. Allsup	Cover	John C. Allsup

OTHER WRITING

One of the aims of this book has been to detail all of Malcolm Saville's original writing, but this has proved to be impossible. For a start, the earliest piece of writing which we can definitely identify is a contribution to *My Garden* magazine in 1934, but we know that he was writing football reviews in the 1930s and they possibly pre-date this. So we seem to have fallen at the first hurdle. Also, given the number of pieces which turned up during the preparation of this book, it seems likely there are more that we have not seen.

We have searched everywhere we can think of, we have talked to every Saville fan we know, we have gone up blind alleys in tracking down half-remembered pieces and what we present here is the best that we can do. If you know of any writing which we have missed, please let us know and we will try and alert other Saville fans to them through *Acksherley!*.

In addition to the original writing, we have also included publications which contain extracts from Malcolm Saville's work. This is a little more subjective since brief quotes are common. For example, he was often asked to provide small quotes for the inside flap of other authors' books. Those that we have included are of a substantial nature or maybe of particular interest.

Malcolm Saville's career as a book author included mostly fiction, but he also wrote a smaller number of non-fiction books. His output outside the books is the other way round and the number of different subjects that are included indicates the range and variety of his interests, many of which permeate the fiction. However it is disappointing that he did not write more short fiction. It is limited to two short stories: one Lone Pine and one Michael and Mary (or two if you include *Where the Bus Stopped*), and two early pieces for *My Garden* magazine. If you have not read them, at least you have these treats to look forward to.

ADVENTURE AND DISCOVERY
FOR BOYS AND GIRLS

This was a series of six rather worthy books published by Cape between 1946 and 1951. Well known contributors included Geoffrey Trease, Ian Serraillier, H E Bates and Chapman Pincher. Malcolm Saville contributed to three of them. As with the later Discovery and Romance for Boys and Girls, the articles are profusely illustrated with what appear to be stock black and white photographs. The exception is the D. J. Desmond piece, where the pictures look to have been especially commissioned.

No 2 1947 **OW 1**   *Guardians of Our Coast* The story of the Coastguard Service.

No 3 1948 **OW 2**   *The World's Greatest Port* The story of London's docks and *Craftsmanship in a Machine Age* (as D. J. Desmond) The story of the men working on the rebuilding of Parliament after World War 2.

No 5 1950 **OW 3**   *London's Fire Fighters* The story of the London Fire Brigade.

ALPHABET ASSEMBLY   OW 4

Published by The Religious Education Press Ltd in 1965, this is an anthology of worship for secondary schools arranged by alphabetical themes and edited by Betty Trew. Malcolm Saville's contribution, under the theme of daring, is an extract from *The Adventure of the Lifeboat Service* about Grace Darling's rescue of the Forfarshire crew.

THE AUTUMN BOOK   OW 5

Within the pages of this book and particularly in this section you will find a number of instances where Malcolm Saville had extracts included in almanacs of poetry and prose and, indeed, he produced several himself. This one was part of a season based series selected by James Reeves and illustrated by Colin McNaughton. It was published by Heinemann in 1977 (ISBN 434 95896 4). The Malcolm Saville extract is *What Jane Saw in October* which you will not be surprised to learn was taken from Jane's Country Year.

BEST CHILDREN'S STORIES OF THE YEAR

This was a series published between about 1946 and 1951 by The Burke Publishing Co featuring extracts from books by children's writers and edited by Leonard Gribble. Two of Malcolm Saville's books were selected and each extract is accompanied by an original colour illustration. We have shown the publication years of the Saville books, but the anthologies may have appeared a year or two later.

No 2 1947
`OW 6`
Rain for St Swithins From *Jane's Country Year*. Illustrated by Margaret Green.

No 3 1948
`OW 7`
The Unwelcome Stranger From The Riddle of the Painted Box. Illustrated by Joan Martin May.

BOOKS AND BOOKMEN   `OW 8`

The December 1958 edition of this literary magazine, published by Hansom Books, featured children's Christmas books. Malcolm Saville is pictured on the front cover and there is an article about him inside. His own contribution is a short piece about how he came to write *King of Kings*.

There is also a small photograph of Malcolm Saville and his son Jeremy on the Stiperstones and advertisements for *King of Kings* and *Secret of the Gorge*.

In December 1965, Malcolm Saville contributes ***Romance, that's what they like*** and gives his ideas of books that children like to read when they choose for themselves, based on over 20 years as a writer.

BOOKS FOR YOUR CHILDREN   `OW 9 SNA`

In the October 1973 edition of this magazine Malcolm Saville contributed ***What children write to me***. He talks about the kind of letters he receives and one is re-produced. He also gives some views on writing for children and on the world in general with his alternative: "The world where quiet kindness and personal unselfishness are not so rare and in which self discipline is still recognised as a virtue".

CHILDREN'S NEWSPAPER

A publication which ran from 1919 – 1965 must have been a success, but it is not remembered fondly and seems to have been what parents bought for their children rather than something the children chose for themselves. Still, it reflects its time and, if you lived through this period, it can make for an interesting read.

Each issue featured a heavily abbreviated text serial by well-known authors. Three of Malcolm Saville's stories were included, each of them before the publication of the book, with the idea perhaps of whetting the children's appetite for the real thing. They are not easy to find but, at the time of writing, all the editions featuring the Malcolm Saville stories can be viewed and downloaded at the Look and Learn website at www.lookandlearn.com.

The Buckinghams at Ravenswyke The serial was in 13 parts and ran between 19 January and 12 April 1952. It was the only story featured without illustrations. The book itself was not published until September of that year.

In the edition for 6 June 1953, under the title The Editor's Table, there is a short piece by Malcolm Saville called **Message of the Coronation** in which he welcomes in the New Elizabethan Age.

Between 14 May and 24 September 1955 **The Secret of Buzzard Scar** was serialised in 20 parts. The final part is accompanied by an advertisement for the forthcoming book, which was published a month later. Each episode had at least one illustration of good quality but these are not credited.

The final serial appeared between 25 January and 7 June 1958, also in 20 episodes. This was **The Secret of the Gorge**, which was first published in book form in September 1958. Again, this is sensitively illustrated but clearly by a different hand.

CHRISTIAN LIBRARIAN

Published by the Librarians' Christian Fellowship, the second issue in 1977 includes the transcript of a talk that Malcolm Saville gave to them on 14 May 1977 at Birmingham Central Library. It was called **Chasing the Sweet Swift Dream** and he talks of his faith and gives his views on society and how children are educated and entertained.

CHURCH STRETTON & SOUTH
SHROPSHIRE RAMBLES OW 12

Robert Smart was a good friend of Malcolm Saville so when Robert published his little book of walks in the Church Stretton area, who better to write an introduction? Malcolm Saville wrote a warm recommendation for the 1978 edition and this can also be found in the 1980 edition but no others. Robert's later book, *Church Stretton Motoring Rambles*, contains an advertisement, in the form of an introduction from Malcolm Saville, for the earlier book.

COUNTRY FAIR OW 13

This magazine covered countryside matters in general and every month there was a feature on a different British county. It cannot be said that Malcolm Saville was a regular contributor, but we have discovered five pieces by him and there are likely to be more.

December 1956 **Christmas Books for Children** Reviews of new children's books by Richmal Crompton and Monica Edwards, among others. Someone else pens the review of Wings over Witchend.

March 1957 **Gardening Books** Reviews of three new books.

June 1957 **A Rosette for Theo A Stephens** A tribute by Malcolm Saville to a man who had been his colleague, his mentor, his boss and his friend for over 30 years.

September 1957 **Book**s More short reviews of gardening and natural history books.

December 1957 **Children's Bookshelf** Christmas again and some more reviews including one for Pat Smythe's first book.

DISCOVERY AND ROMANCE
FOR GIRLS AND BOYS

These books are very similar to the Adventure and Discovery series, but perhaps aimed more at girls. Again published by Cape, it may have only been produced for three years. The two Malcolm Saville articles cover similar ground.

No 2 1947 **The Eternal Romance of Farming** A tribute to Britain's farmers.
`OW 14`

No 3 1948 **The Story of Milk** The title says it all. Perhaps not Malcolm Saville's
`OW 15` most interesting piece of work.

ENGLISH IN ACTION `OW 16`

This was a five volume set of educational text books published by The University of London and written by Gordon Humphreys and John Roberts. Book three (1963) contains *A Story of Heroism from Scotland*, taken from *Seaside Scrap-Book for Girls and Boys*, and some exercises based on it.

THE GUIDE GIFT BOOK `OW 17`

Before there were *Girl Guide Annuals* there was The Guide Gift Book, a one off publication from The Girl Guide Association in 1950. It contains **The Flower-show Hat**; the only Lone Pine short story, later re-published by The Malcolm Saville Society, with its two Bertram Prance illustrations. The book also contains stories by Ian Serraillier, Geoffrey Trease and Violet Needham, amongst others.

This is an important book for Lone Pine collectors, but is fairly rare. We have seen four different colour boards: beige, light green, dark red and yellow; the latter (the most common) achieves a pleasing mottled yellow/orange effect over the years. The book comes in a predominantly yellow dustjacket.

HOLIDAY GUIDE TO HASTINGS,
ST LEONARDS AND DISTRICT `OW 18`

Malcolm Saville wrote a lovely foreword to this guidebook for the town where he was born and speaks of his intention to return to the area one day. Sadly, it was where he died in 1982. The book was published in 1951 by Adams & Sons of Rye and may have been sold for some years as copies are often found with the Festival of Britain page removed.

Other items of interest in the book are a unique advertisement for the Lone Pine Books and one for Brooker & Saville, the family business.

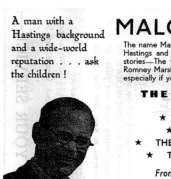
JOHN O'LONDON'S

John O'London's Weekly was a very popular, fairly highbrow, literary magazine which was named after one of its original contributors and was published by Newnes from 1919 to 1954. It re-appeared as John O'London's in 1959 trying to reach a wider audience, but finally expired at the end of 1962.

Malcolm Saville was a regular contributor for the last two years of the magazine's life reviewing children's books, most often in a series called ***Reading for Pleasure***. He appears on the front cover of two editions: 19 October 1961 and 8 November 1962.

JUNIOR RADIO TIMES

For a brief period the Radio Times had a supplement featuring children's programmes on radio and television. In Radio Times volume 145 number 1880 which covered the week beginning November 22 1959, Malcolm Saville wrote a short piece about *The Buckinghams at Ravenswyke* which was to be serialised in ***Children's Hour*** starting at 5:25pm on Saturday 28 November.

THE LASTING VICTORIES

Published by Lutterworth in 1948, this is a book which celebrates achievement both great and small. It was edited by Peter Scott and includes contributions from some well known people and some lesser lights. We have heard of Malcolm Campbell, Chips Rafferty, Bernard Leach and Alexander Fleming. The piece by Malcolm Saville is called **Warriors of the Sea** and is a tribute to the RNLI. It is illustrated with two black and white photographs of lifeboats in action. There is also a piece by his friend Theo Stephens called A Dream Come True in which he talks about his career in publishing and his success in producing *My Garden* magazine.

LIVERPOOL CATHEDRAL
CORONATION SOUVENIR

In a news item in *The Children's Newspaper* of 23 May 1953, they report that Malcolm Saville has been asked by the Bishop of Liverpool to contribute a message in a souvenir booklet to be given to all children visiting the cathedral in Coronation year. We have been unable to confirm it was ever published, but it is hard to believe that he would not have produced the piece. We approached the archivist at the cathedral who could not find a copy of the booklet, though she did say that the archive was being "re-organised". Possibly this was a euphemism and might suggest that they generally have difficulty finding things!

MACDONALD HASTINGS'
COUNTRY BOOK

Published by Newnes in 1961, this is a selection of poems and prose chosen by the well known writer and covering country themes. Under the chapter called *Ploughing*, Hasting includes **The First Storm of Autumn** by Malcolm Saville which had originally been published in *Country Scrap-book for Boys & Girls*.

Hastings was the editor of Country Fair and had published several pieces by Malcolm Saville a few years earlier. It is interesting to note that Malcolm Saville did not return the favour in his own selection, *Words for all Seasons*.

MALCOLM SAVILLE'S NEWSLETTER OW 24

From 1971 until his death in 1982 Malcolm Saville produced his own newsletter which was sent to those interested in his books. They contained news of new books he had written and others that were being re-published. There were 25 in all, numbered 1-23 and 25 with a final un-numbered issue simply titled Book *News from Malcolm Saville*. Number 24 does not exist. After number 19 the title changes to just *Newsletter*.

As the years went by, the tone changed as his books seemed to go out of fashion and the quality of the publication reduced too. Numbers 1-8 were well printed (by ELB printers) and contained some unique character portraits. Then the quality went down; numbers 9-13 had a photograph of Malcolm Saville but then there were no illustrations. Up to issue 23 there were two A4 size pages stapled together and printed both sides. Number 25 is one sheet of A4 double sided and the final issue is one sheet of A5 printed on a single side.

They are difficult to find now and can be expensive. The idea was that each time you received a copy you could send a coupon and a stamp back to receive the next copy. Issues 2-8 were accompanied by a separate coupon but other issues had the coupon incorporated. Consequently, copies are often found with the bottom part of the back page missing.

MEET YOUR AUTHORS OW 25

Over to MALCOLM SAVILLE

Eric Leyland was the editor of this 1963 publication from George G Harrap and Co. It features ten well-known children's writers and each gets a two-page biography, a list of some current books in print, a photograph and an extract from one of their books. The authors are Anthony Buckeridge, Jack Cox, Richmal Crompton, Winifred Finlay, Garry Hogg, Captain W. E. Johns, Eric Leyland, John Pudney, Noel Streatfeild and, of course, Malcolm Saville.

The Saville extract is taken from *Sea Witch Comes Home* and describes the exciting evacuation at the height of the storm. It is titled **Crisis** and is part of chapter XIII and the whole of chapter XIV of the book.

We have seen two versions of the book: one has green boards and has a dustjacket, the design of which is used on the other, laminated edition.

The laminated version is presumably aimed at schools for it contains an extra section at the back called 'Projects' which suggests some essays based on the extracts in the book. Perhaps you would like to have a go at one of these:

Carefully re-read the account of the great storm and then write a newspaper report, including headlines. First study the technique used by journalists in any popular newspaper, noticing how any account is broken up and how headings are used. Remember that such a report must be pithy and eye-catching.

Perhaps James Wilson or Dan Sturt could give you a hand!

MICKEY MOUSE WEEKLY OW 26

This was a British comic which ran from 1936 to 1957 and was published by Odhams. Malcolm Saville's contributions were all in the 1950s and in this period, as well as colour strip cartoons featuring Disney characters, there were also non-Disney black and white strips and text stories. Three Saville stories were serialised and he also wrote a special piece for the Coronation in 1953.

 Lone Pine Five A serial version of the story in 24 parts between 15 March and 23 August 1952. The story usually covered less than one page so was heavily abridged. It featured unique illustrations signed 'Gaffron': probably H C Gaffron.

Secret in the Mist This is a picture strip version of Two Fair Plaits and it ran for eleven episodes between 15 November 1952 and 24 January 1953. The story is mostly told in dialogue with a few pieces of text description and, though savagely abridged, may have whetted children's appetites for the real thing. The illustrations are not credited, though some have specu- lated that they are the work of A R Whitear.

A Little Girl becomes our Queen Mickey Mouse is banished from the front page for the Souvenir Coronation Issue of 30 May 1953 to be replaced by a montage of Corona- tion images. Malcolm Saville tells the story of the childhood of Elizabeth and extols the qualities that would make her a good Queen in a full page article illustrated by photo- graphs.

 Seven White Gates Another Lone Pine story is serialised, this time in eighteen episodes between 5 December 1953 and 3 April 1954, with illus- trations by F Stocks May. In our opinion, the illustrations for this serial are amongst the best ever produced for any of Malcolm Saville's work.

MY GARDEN AN INTIMATE MAGAZINE FOR GARDEN LOVERS

Theo A Stephens was the driving force behind this high quality little magazine which first appeared in January 1934 and ran for 216 editions until December 1951. Stephens seems to have been a mentor to Malcolm Saville and they were friends from the late 1920s. *The Buckinghams at Ravenswyke* was dedicated to him. He was also Managing Director of C Arthur Pearson Ltd, who published *Amateur Acting and Producing for Beginners* and was on the board of Newnes where Malcolm Saville was employed.

The magazine was published from offices in Southampton Street in London for most of its life, but in 1949 Stephens acquired a large house (with garden) in Guildford and publication continued from there. Malcolm Saville moved to Guildford too.

Malcolm Saville's first contribution was as early as the third issue in 1934 and his early pieces showed only the initials MS. Later, he would use his pseudonym of D. J. Desmond. After the war he was a regular contributor, often editing the magazine in Stephens' absence and being shown as Associate Editor from January 1948.

Major Contributions

March 1934 **The Soldier's Garden** by MS. A short story really, about a soldier's family and the difficulties of establishing a garden when they are constantly on the move. This is Malcolm Saville's earliest identified published writing.

May 1934 **Gardens in the Air** by MS. About the gardens of our imagination.

February 1935 **The Arts of War in a Garden** by A Soldier's Wife (but initialled MS). More about the soldier and his family as they buy a new home and create a garden.

April 1939 **Stonewall Jackson** Written as D. J. Desmond, Thomas Jackson is the kind of gardener which the writer cannot find in later stories.

November 1939 **The Flowers Must Stay** Written as D. J. Desmond. An argument for retaining flowers in gardens at a time when people were being urged to cultivate more vegetables.

August 1940 **To Any American Father From An English Father** A plea to the Americans to take good care of British evacuated children.

September 1946 **Jealous Flowers** A short article which talks about the emotional life of flowers.

January 1947 **My Gardeners I – Smithson** The first in a series of three illustrated short stories, possibly autobiographical.

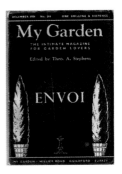

March 1947 **My Gardeners II – Charlie** The second humorous story in the series and the illustrations, as in the other two, are not credited.

October 1947 **My Gardeners III – Meadows** The third of the series features another fruitless attempt to employ a good gardener.

July 1949 **Chelsea in Retrospect** A personal review of the Chelsea Flower Show where the magazine had its own stand.

July 1950 **Chelsea in Retrospect** Another wet week in Chelsea for Malcolm Saville to review, but he clearly had a very good time meeting old friends.

December 1951 **We Carried the Torch**. In the final issue, Malcolm Saville takes a wistful look back at the history of the magazine.

During the post war period Theo Stephens took a number of trips abroad and also had a spell in hospital. Malcolm Saville edited the magazine in his absence. His editorials are well worth reading and appear in the editions for April 1947, May 1947, March 1948, May 1948, February 1949, March 1949, April 1949 and March 1951.

He was also the book reviewer for the magazine, mostly on gardening books. His reviews appear in the editions for August 1946, February 1947, December 1948, August 1949, January 1951, April 1951 and in the seven issues from May to November 1951 where they were titled *My Garden's Bookshelf*.

The initials MS appear frequently in the magazine, most notably in a miscellany column called My Garden's Notebook in every issue from June 1947 to December 1951.

In the August 1950 edition there is a photograph of the executives of the magazine including both Theo Stephens and a very dapper looking Malcolm Saville.

My Garden also published a number of books throughout its life. Of particular interest are *My Garden's Good-Night* published in 1939, which reprinted both *The Arts of War in a Garden* and *Stonewall Jackson*, and *My Garden's Bedside Book* from 1950, which reprised *My Gardener Smithson*. Very keen collectors may be interested in the 1949 book *Bringing the Garden Indoors* by Sheila Pim which was illustrated by David Saville, Malcolm's younger brother.

`OW 28`
`OW 29`

READ ALOUD TALES FROM
SUNNY STORIES

`OW 30`

Malcolm Saville was the editor of the Sunny Stories comic from 1954 to 1958 and during this time a number of books appeared under the overall title of Sunny Stories Bookshelf. It can be conjectured that he may have had responsibility for choosing the stories for them all, but the only one in which he is named as editor is *Read Aloud Tales*, which was published by Newnes in 1956. He pens a short editorial in which he encourages parents and teachers to read stories to children.

THE RUN

`OW 31`

This is the most obscure piece of Malcolm Saville's writing which we have come across and the purists would probably argue that it does not warrant a place in this book.

Bowmandale County Primary School is in Barton-Upon-Humber and they decided that the children would write a book based on a story which they had been researching concerning smugglers and the murder of a solder in Staithes in North Yorkshire.

Malcolm Saville was invited to the school in March 1981 and he met the children and staff and gave them the benefit of his professional advice. The result was a little comb-bound book that appeared later in the year complete with a foreward by him in which he congratulates them on their efforts and encourages them to continue writing.

SHROPSHIRE MAGAZINE

`OW 32`

Many English counties have their own magazine and Shropshire's has been published since the late 1940s. As an adopted son of the county, Malcolm Saville gets frequent mentions but his only known contribution is **What Shropshire Means to Me** in the

December 1956 edition. In this he tells of his love for Shropshire and describes his first journey there in 1936. He mentions the settings for his Shropshire- based books and he also confirms Prior's Holt as the inspiration for Witchend calling it "a not very attractive house with stabling". The piece is accompanied by a poem by Monica Bott called *Stretton Hills*.

SIX OF THE BEST OW 33

Where the Bus Stopped

Malcolm Saville

BASIL BLACKWELL
OXFORD
1966

The most difficult to find of all Malcolm Saville's books is ***Where the Bus Stopped*** which is really only a short story and is contained in this anthology published by Blackwells in 1955 and edited by the well known children's author: Geoffrey Trease.

The book contains six stories by well-known authors and each one was also published in book form. Trease himself contributed a story and the others are by Cynthia Hartnett, Wilfrid Robertson and Stephen Tring.

They are all scarce so putting the sequence together has been difficult, but it seems that both the anthology and individual books were dated 1956, 1959, 1964 and 1966. The anomalies were that the 1956 versions of the small books were actually issued in 1955 and the boards were paper covered, the 1959 versions all had page numbers taken from the anthology and the 1964 and 1966 versions showed the copyright date as 1959. It looks as though all the books were issued to schools only, thus the scarcity.

Experience suggests that it is slightly easier to obtain the anthology so it is worth looking for if you want to read *Where the Bus Stopped*.

SOMETHING OF SUSSEX OW 34

This is a book of black and white photographs by Vera Garner Howe, published by W.E. Baxter Ltd in 1959 and with an introduction by Malcolm Saville dated January of that year. In it he talks of his love of Sussex and what it means to him. In his introduction to the Hastings Guidebook in 1951 he had described himself as a Sussex exile but by 1959 he was living in Barcombe, back in the county of his birth and would stay there for the rest of his life.

SONG OF THE MORNING

Compiled by Pat Alexander and published simultaneously in Britain, the USA and Australia in 1997, this is an anthology of stories and poems for Easter and includes pieces by writers such as C S Lewis, G K Chesterton and Eleanor Farjeon. Malcolm Saville's piece was titled *Jesus' Last Week Begins* and is an extract from *King of Kings*. It is illustrated with a drawing by Robin Lawrie. A paperback version followed in the UK in 1999.

The hardback versions were published by Lion in the UK (ISBN 0 7459 3209 6) and the US (0 7459 3742 X) but in Australia by Albatross Books (0 7324 1223 4). Lion also published the paperback (0 7459 3951 1).

STORY TROVE

This was another book from the Burke Publishing Company that featured extracts from popular books of the time. It is dated 1950 and includes such well known writers as Noel Streatfeild, Enid Blyton, Barbara Euphan Todd and Captain W E Johns. Malcolm Saville contributes *A Strange Couple* which is taken from chapter three of Lone Pine Five and features Jenny and Mr Wilkins. It has been edited, presumably so that it can stand alone, and contains a Bertram Prance illustration which did not appear in the original book.

SUNNY STORIES

Published by Newnes, Sunny Stories for Little Folks started in July 1926 and was apparently written entirely by Enid Blyton until 1953. In 1937 it was renamed Enid Blyton's Sunny Stories and ran under that name until she left, when it was abbreviated to Sunny Stories. It was briefly edited by the former royal nanny Marion Crawford (Crawfie) and then by Malcolm Saville from 1 November 1954 to 24 March 1958. It struggled on with unnamed editors into the 1960s.

Sunny Stories was aimed at younger children and was a mix of stories, puzzles, competitions, etc. It has been suggested that Enid Blyton left because she was not allowed to advertise her books in Sunny Stories so it is interesting to see that the occasional advertisement for a Malcolm Saville title does appear when he was editor.

Some of the contributors were quite well known writers such as Arthur Groom but many are not so familiar. Malcolm Saville is not known to have written any stories for the magazine but it is difficult to believe that he did not contribute. It has been speculated that Molly Sole could have been a Malcolm Saville pseudonym, but there is no real proof of this. Editorials are penned under the name Sunny Sam and this is presumably Malcolm Saville.

For Club Members Only

SUNNY STORIES
CLUB NEWS

THE WONDER BOOK FOR CHILDREN

Malcolm Saville wrote many short pieces but there are only two short stories featuring characters from his series books. The story here is **Harvest Holiday** and features the return of Michael and Mary Bishop to Townsend Farm a year after their adventures in *Trouble at Townsend*.

The story is crammed with twenty illustrations by Lunt Roberts which is the same number as he produced for the much longer *Trouble at Townsend*. The frontispiece to the whole book is a splendid colour illustration by him of a harvest supper.

The book is a compendium of short stories and was published by Odhams in 1948. Various versions are known to exist. The Wonder Book for Children has a brightly illustrated dustjacket and the book has burgundy coloured boards with gold block. Another version shows *The Daily Herald Wonder Book for Children* on the jacket but has the basic title both inside and outside the book. The boards are green with black block and have illustrations on the front and spine.

Malcolm Saville was a very popular children's writer over a long period so it is not surprising that his work was published abroad. He did not have any great success in the biggest market of all, the USA, but appears to have been quite successful in Europe and Australia. The Lone Pine books were the most popular but most of the series achieved some recognition outside the UK. In all, 40 titles were published overseas and in nine foreign languages.

There were not many foreign editions that were published in English, but this is a bit misleading. Malcolm Saville was popular in the English speaking British Empire/ Commonwealth and clearly these countries simply imported the books.

For the collector foreign editions can be a particularly rewarding area as there is no definitive list and there is still the possibility of discovering a new edition. For this bibliography we have listed editions which we definitely know to exist. In all, there are sixty-eight books, and as we are writing this, we have sixty of them to hand. Of the other eight, one we have seen and the other seven have turned up consistently in internet searches, all in libraries and not for sale.

The two non-English speaking countries where Malcolm Saville was most popular were Spain and Holland. The Spanish books are becoming very collectable in both Britain and Spain. It is good to see that as late as 2008 there were re-issues of some Dutch paperbacks.

There remain three books which might exist. They were identified in Mark O'Hanlon's trawl through the records of Malcolm Saville's literary agent and were clearly planned. These were Swedish editions of *Wings over Witchend* and *Man with Three Fingers* and a *Norwegian Mystery at Witchend*. In addition, we have seen several references to Icelandic translations but can find only one.

The translations are a guide and are the best we can do. Our apologies go to the linguists amongst our readers who may be horrified at the omission of the odd accent, umlaut or tilde.

AUSTRALIA

The first five Lone Pine books were published by Dymock's Book Exchange Ltd of Sydney. Internally they are very similar to the early Newnes editions. The boards are a little different though; they are green with black block and a pine tree on both spine and front. All the illustrations (including jackets) are by Bertram Prance and are the same as Newnes, but with different descriptive material on the dustjackets.

There are rumours of an Australian edition of The Elusive Grasshopper, possibly by a different publisher, but we have not been able to track a copy down.

The Gay Dolphin Adventure	1952 Hardback	FE 1
Lone Pine Five	1951 Hardback	FE 2
Mystery at Witchend	1951 Hardback	FE 3
The Secret of Grey Walls	1952 Hardback	FE 4
Seven White Gates	1951 Hardback	FE 5

CANADA

Only one Canadian edition is known to exist and what a strange title for them to have chosen. *The Thin Grey Man* is not one of Malcolm Saville's better-known books and the UK editions are not easy to find.

The publisher is based in St John's Newfoundland and is probably the most obscure of all those who published Malcolm Saville's work. We have seen this book listed as *The Thin Gray Man* but this seems to be an error; the copies we have seen have the correct title.

The Thin Grey Man			FE 6
Publisher	Breakwater Books	Year/Type	1981 Paperback
Translator	N/A	ISBN	0 919948 17 0
Notes		All the Desmond Knight illustrations are retained and the cover features a black and white version of his Grasshopper cover illustration.	

FINLAND

The Finns were late converts to Malcolm Saville. Three of the first four Lone Pines were published in hardback in the late 1980s/ early 1990s. It is surprising that *The Secret of Grey Walls* was not published but, as the three known titles appear in a number of Finnish library catalogues, it seems unlikely it was. But you never know! The publisher was Karisto of Hämeenlinna and all three books are laminated hardbacks. They all contain the original maps translated into Finnish but none have illustrations. The cover pictures, which are wraparound and may be by the same illustrator, are not credited.

The Gay Dolphin Adventure — FE 7

Foreign Title	Iloisen Delfiinin Majatalo (The Inn of a Happy Dolphin)		
Publisher	Karisto	Year/Type	1991 Laminated
Translator	Laila Rauhamaa	ISBN	951 23 3008 3

Mystery at Witchend — FE 8

Foreign Title	Seikkailu Alkaa (The Adventure Begins)		
Publisher	Karisto	Year/Type	1989 Laminated
Translator	Auli Hurme-Keränen	ISBN	951 23 2629-9

Seven White Gates — FE 9

Foreign Title	Seitsemän Valkoista Porttia (Seven White Gates)		
Publisher	Karisto	Year/Type	1990 Laminated
Translator	Auli Hurme-Kernen	ISBN	951 23 2819-4

FRANCE

The three titles published in France may seem odd choices, but the Marston Baines stories are both set in Europe so maybe they are not too surprising. Interestingly, they include the only Marston Baines paperbacks.

Three Towers in Tuscany   FE 10

Foreign Title	Bill Marston Contre Inconnus (Bill Marston against Strangers)		
Publisher	Hachette	Year/Type	1972 Paperback
Translator	Paul Verguin.	ISBN	20 6003 6
Notes	There are no text illustrations and the cover is not credited.		

Two Fair Plaits   FE 11

Foreign Title	Deux Tresses Blondes (Two Fair Plaits)		
Publisher	Editions Gautier-Languereau	Year/Type	1962 Laminated
Translator	Yvonne Girault	ISBN	No
Notes	Illustrations by Francoise Bertier, cover not credited.		

White Fire   FE 12

Foreign Title	Bill Marston et les disparus de Majorque (Bill Marston and the Vanished Ones of Majorca)		
Publisher	Hachette	Year/Type	1972 Paperback
Translator	Jean Muray	ISBN	20 6012 7
Notes	There are no text illustrations and the cover is not credited.		

GERMANY

It is possibly not surprising that British fiction was not popular in the post-war years in Germany and none of Malcolm Saville's fiction titles were translated into German. Kathy Wyatt's illustrations are retained.

King of Kings   FE 13

Foreign Title	Der Sohn des Zimmermanns (The Son of a Carpenter)		
Publisher	R. Brockhaus Verlag	Year/Type	1978 Hardback
Translator	Not Known	ISBN	3 417 12618 5
Notes	Cover design by Ralf Rudolph, photograph by David Alexander.		

HOLLAND

Second only to the Spanish in the number of titles produced, the Dutch have enjoyed Malcolm Saville books for more than 50 years. The re-issue of two paperbacks in 2008 also means they have by far the most recent foreign editions. As with most countries, the Lone Pine books are most popular, but the Jillies get a look-in as well and they produced the first paperback version of *Treasure at the Mill*, which pre-dates its British equivalent by five years.

The Gay Dolphin Adventure   FE 14

Foreign Title	Het geheim van de oude herberg (The Secret of the Old Inn)		
Publisher	Het Spectrum	Year/Type	1963 Paperback
Translator	S Horrev-orts-Hueber	ISBN	No
Notes	The excellent and very foreign cover is signed DELEEUW and, although there are no text illustrations, there is a re-drawn map.		

The Gay Dolphin Adventure   FE 15

Foreign Title	Het geheim van de oude herberg (The Secret of the Old Inn)		
Publisher	Disney's Juniorclub	Year/Type	1984 Laminated
Translator	S Horrev-oets-Hueber	ISBN	90 320 3355 7
Notes	The cover is not credited and there are no illustrations or maps.		

Lone Pine Five   FE 16

Foreign Title	roman treasure		
Publisher	P Noordhoff Ltd	Year/Type	Unknown/Paperback
Translator	G. van Veelo	ISBN	N/A
Notes	Abridged school English reader with translations into Dutch.		

The Luck of Sallowby

Foreign Title	De jacht op de talisman (The Hunt for the Amulet) FE 17		
Publisher	Het Spectrum	Year/Type	1960 Paperback
Translator	M. Schooneveldt-Salm	ISBN	N/A
Notes	The cover is not credited but the original Tilden Reeves illustrations are included together with a translated version of the original map.		

The Luck of Sallowby
FE 18

Foreign Title	De jacht op de talisman (The Hunt for the Amulet)		
Publisher	Disney's Juniorclub	Year/Type	1984 Laminated
Translator	M. Schoone-veldt-Salm	ISBN	90 320 3255 0
Notes	The cover is not credited and there are no illustrations or maps.		

Mystery at Witchend
FE 19

Foreign Title	Raadsels om de Heksenhoek (Mystery at Witch Corner)		
Publisher	Bel Junior	Year/Type	1959 Paperback
Translator	J Baas-van Dijk	ISBN	N/A
Notes	The cover and eight black and white illustrations are by R van Looy,		

Mystery at Witchend
FE 20

Foreign Title	Raadsels om de Heksenhoek (Mystery at Witch Corner)		
Publisher	Het Spectrum	Year/Type	1962 Paperback
Translator	J Baas-van Dijk	ISBN	N/A
Notes	The cover is by Frise and there is a re-drawn map in Dutch but no other illustrations.		

Redshank's Warning
FE 21

Foreign Title	De Jillies op dievenjacht (The Jillies on the Hunt for Thieves)		
Publisher	Het Spectrum	Year/Type	1962 Paperback
Translator	C F Boltje-Beets	ISBN	N/A
Notes	Contains the original map (translated) and Lunt Roberts illustration but the cover illustrations is not credited.		

The Secret of Grey Walls
FE 22

Foreign Title	Het Geheim van het eenzame huis (Secret of the Lonesome House)		
Publisher	Het Spectrum	Year/Type	1963 Paperback
Translator	J Baas-van Dijk	ISBN	N/A
Notes	The cover is not credited but the original Prance illustrations and a translated version of the original map are included. The book was re-issued in 2008 with an ISBN number 9789031501762. Virtually the same as the original (so the blurb on the back advertises out of print books) but better quality paper.		

Seven White Gates

Foreign Title	Het geheim van de zeven witte hekken (The Secret of the Seven White Gates		
Publisher	Bel Junior	Year/Type	1959 Paperback
Translator	J Baas-van Dijk	ISBN	N/A
Notes	The cover and eight black and white illustrations are by R van Looy. There is no map.		

Seven White Gates

Foreign Title	Het Geheim van de zeven witte hekken (The Secret of the Seven White Gates)		
Publisher	Prisma	Year/Type	1962 Paperback
Translator	J Baas-van Dijk	ISBN	N/A
Notes	The Bertram Prance illustrations are included and a miniature, translated, version of the original map. Re-issued in 2008 with an ISBN number 9789031501755. Better quality paper but otherwise much the same as the original.		

Treasure at the Mill

Foreign Title	De schat in de watermolen (Treasure in the Water Mill)		
Publisher	Prisma	Year/Type	1959 Paperback
Translator	A K W Wolsak-van Dorp	ISBN	N/A
Notes	The cover is not credited but Harry Pettit's illustrations are, as are his map (now in Dutch) and plan of the mill.		

Two Fair Plaits

Foreign Title	Ontvoering in de mist (Abduction in the Mist)		
Publisher	Prisma	Year/Type	1961 Paperback
Translator	S D Houtsma - van Schaik	ISBN	N/A
Notes	Cover is by C W Voges and most of Lunt Roberts' original illustrations are included, as is the map which is now in Dutch.		

ICELAND

A late trawl through the records of Malcolm Saville's literary agents brought an Icelandic book to light. It is rare and we have traced only two copies - one with no cover picture and the other where we have found a black and white scan of a presumably colour cover picture. This suggests it is a hardback edition.

The Secret of the Villa Rosa		FE 27
Foreign Title	Leyndardómur Villa Rosa (Secret Villa Rosa)	
Publisher	Örn og Örlygur	Year/Type	1972 Hardback
Translator	Eiríkur Tómasson	ISBN	N/A
Notes	No illustrator (if any) details known.	

NORWAY

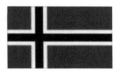

It could hardly be said that Malcolm Saville made much of a splash in Norway. You would have thought that with all those long winter nights they would have enjoyed nothing better than to read about children tramping round Shropshire on long wet summer days, but the Lone Piners did not make it this far north. Only the Jillies and then, two decades later, Marston Baines.

The Purple Valley		FE 28
Foreign Title	Den Hemmelige Dalen (The Purple Valley)	
Publisher	Greig	Year/Type	1973 Hardback
Translator	Mossa Sverre	ISBN	82 533 0087 5
Notes	No text illustrations and the dustjacket is not credited.	

Redshank's Warning		FE 29
Foreign Title	Varselsfuglen (Warning bird)	
Publisher	Aschehoug	Year/Type	1951 Hardback
Translator	Anders Hagerup	ISBN	N/A
Notes	There are no text illustrations and no dustjacket has surfaced but the illustrated cover features an uncredited and very unusual looking redshank.	

Three Towers in Tuscany			**FE 30**
Foreign Title	Farlig Ferie (Dangerous Holiday)		
Publisher	Greig	Year/Type	1973 Hardback
Translator	Mossa Sverre	ISBN	82 533 0151 0
Notes	No text illustrations and the very garish dustjacket is not credited.		

Two Fair Plaits			**FE 31**
Foreign Title	To Lyse Fletter (Two Fair Plaits)		
Publisher	Aschehoug	Year/Type	1952 Hardback
Translator	Anders Hagerup	ISBN	N/A
Notes	The book has a picture cover that is not credited and just one of the original Lunt Roberts illustrations. We have not seen a dustjacket.		

PORTUGAL

All eight Susan and Bill titles were published by Inquerito of Lisbon and are very difficult to find. Most of our information comes from library records.

The books are slightly different from the UK paperbacks as they have flaps which are similar to dustjackets. The covers all feature elegant illustrations by Infante do Carmo, each with a different predominant pastel shade, and the books retain the original frontispieces by Ernest Shepard or T R Freeman as well as their text illustrations, but the latter have been shaded in various pastel colours.

The series is called *Aventuras de Susana and Guilherme* and all the books were translated by José Parreira Alves. They are undated but probably all 1960.

Susan, Bill and the Bright Star Circus		**FE 32**
Foreign Title	O Circo Ambulante (The Travelling Circus)	

Susan, Bill and the Dark Stranger		**FE 33**
Foreign Title	O Homem de Preto (The Man in Black)	

Susan, Bill and the Golden Clock		**FE 34 SNA**
Foreign Title	O Relógio Dourado (The Golden Watch)	

Susan, Bill and the Ivy Clad Oak		**FE 35**
Foreign Title	O Roble Secular (The Centenary Tree)	

	Susan, Bill and the Pirates Bold	FE 36
Foreign Title	As Férias Maravilhosas (The Wonderful Holiday)	

	Susan, Bill and the Saucy Kate	FE 37
Foreign Title	A Praia Das Surpresas (The Beach of Surprises)	

	Susan, Bill and the Vanishing Boy	FE 38
Foreign Title	O Rapaz Fugitivo (The Fugitive Boy)	

	Susan, Bill and the Wolf Dog	FE 39
Foreign Title	O Cão Lobo (The Wolf Dog)	

SPAIN

The Spanish Lone Pine books must have a special mention. They were published by Molino of Barcelona and are all in hardback. They are similar in size to Newnes editions, but have picture covers and the back of the books show a parchment with the names of the Lone Piners listed. The parchments are not updated when Harriet joins and an interesting error in some editions is that the club captain is listed as David John Sterling.

All the books are in the Adventura Series which features mostly Saville and Enid Blyton titles. The end sheets of all the books have the same illustration of two silhouetted children reading, shaded in various colours; we have seen different colours used for the same titles, though there are no other indications that the books are different editions.

The dustjackets are particularly interesting. The front and back are the same as the book covers and the flaps and, unusually, the inside of these double-sided jackets are used as advertisements for other Molino titles. There are variations in these jackets too. We have seen two versions of several titles. This does not affect the front or back, but the advertising material on the flaps and inside are updated.

They used the Bertram Prance illustrations for the first eight titles, but then brought in local artists to provide original illustrations for most of the rest. All the dustjacket illustrations are by Spanish artists. Unfortunately most of the books do not have maps.

As this bibliography progressed we were adding titles and reached the point where we know that the first 18 Lone Pine titles were published by Molino. It is possible Molino published the final two Lone Pine titles, but we now think it unlikely.

The ISBN numbers quoted are shown in a number of Spanish library sites. We have included them here to help in locating the books but we have only seen them on one book (*Strangers at Witchend*). This suggests there are later reprints of a number of the titles.

All Summer Through   FE 40

Foreign Title	El Club de los Lechuzos (The Owls Club)		
Publisher	Molino	Year/Type	1964 Hardback
Translator	Maria Delores Raich	ISBN	84 272 3045 1
Illustrator	Joan Kiddell-Monroe	Cover/Jacket	Pablo Ramírez

The Elusive Grasshopper   FE 41

Foreign Title	El Saltamontes Esquivo (The Elusive Grasshopper)		
Publisher	Molino	Year/Type	1965 Hardback
Translator	Enrique De Obregon	ISBN	84 272 3057 5
Illustrator	Bertram Prance	Cover/Jacket	Pablo Ramírez
Notes	There is a re-drawn map in Spanish.		

The Gay Dolphin Adventure   FE 42

Foreign Title	Aventura en el Gay Dolphin (Adventure at the Gay Dolphin)		
Publisher	Molino	Year/Type	1963 Hardback
Translator	Ramon Margalef Llambrich	ISBN	84 272 3039 7
Illustrator	Bertram Prance	Cover/Jacket	Pablo Ramírez

Lone Pine Five   FE 43

Foreign Title	Los Cinco del Pino Solitario (Lone Pine Five)		
Publisher	Molino	Year/Type	1964 Hardback
Translator	Enrique De Obregon	ISBN	84 272 3046 X
Illustrator	Bertram Prance	Cover/Jacket	Pablo Ramírez

Lone Pine London   FE 44

Foreign Title	El Misterio de los Falsificadores (The Mystery of the Forgers)		
Publisher	Molino	Year/Type	1967 Hardback
Translator	M L Pol de Ramirez	ISBN	84 272 3075 3
Illustrator	None	Cover/Jacket	Badia Camps

Man with Three Fingers `FE 45`

Foreign Title	El Hombre de los Tres Dedos (The Man with Three Fingers)		
Publisher	Molino	Year/Type	1970 Hardback
Translator	M. Giménez	ISBN	84 272 3105 9
Illustrator	José Ma Bea	Cover/Jacket	Badía Camps

Mystery at Witchend `FE 46`

Foreign Title	El Club del Pino Solitaro (The Lone Pine Club)		
Publisher	Molino	Year/Type	1961 Hardback
Translator	Juan García Guerrero	ISBN	84 272 3024 9
Illustrator	Bertram Prance	Cover/Jacket	Pablo Ramírez

Mystery Mine `FE 47`

Foreign Title	Misterio en la Mina (Mystery in the Mine)		
Publisher	Molino	Year/Type	1969 Hardback
Translator	M L Pol de Ramirez	ISBN	84 272 3090 7
Illustrator	Carlos Giménez	Cover/Jacket	Badía Camps

The Neglected Mountain `FE 48`

Foreign Title	La Montaña Abandonada (The Abandoned Mountain)		
Publisher	Molino	Year/Type	1965 Hardback
Translator	Enrique De Obregon	ISBN	84 272 3059 1
Illustrator	Bertram Prance	Cover/Jacket	Pablo Ramírez
Notes	There are two re-drawn maps in Spanish.		

Not Scarlet But Gold `FE 49`

Foreign Title	Misterio en la Cañada (Mystery in the Gully)		
Publisher	Molino	Year/Type	1969 Hardback
Translator	M L Pol de Ramirez	ISBN	84 272 3096 6
Illustrator	Escolano	Cover/Jacket	Badía Camps

Rye Royal `FE 50`

Foreign Title	El Secreto de Rye Royal (The Secret of Rye Royal)		
Publisher	Molino	Year/Type	1971 Hardback
Translator	M. Giménez	ISBN	84 272 3107 5
Illustrator	José Ma Bea	Cover/Jacket	Badía Camps

Saucers over the Moor

Foreign Title	Misterio de los Platillos Volantes (Mystery of the Flying Saucers)		
Publisher	Molino	Year/Type	1965 Hardback
Translator	M L Pol de Ramirez	ISBN	84 272 3065 6
Illustrator	Bertram Prance	Cover/Jacket	Badía Camps

Sea Witch comes Home

Foreign Title	El Regreso de la "Bruja del Mar" (The Return of the "Witch of the Sea")		
Publisher	Molino	Year/Type	1969 Hardback
Translator	M L Pol de Ramirez	ISBN	84 272 3093 1
Illustrator	Escolano	Cover/Jacket	Badía Camps

The Secret of Grey Walls

Foreign Title	El Secreto de Grey Walls (The Secret of Grey Walls)		
Publisher	Molino	Year/Type	1963 Hardback
Translator	Enrique De Obregon	ISBN	84 272 3041 9
Illustrator	Bertram Prance	Cover/Jacket	Badia Camps

The Secret of the Gorge

Foreign Title	El Secreto del Barranco (The Secret of the Gorge)		
Publisher	Molino	Year/Type	1968 Hardback
Translator	Miguel Gimenez Sales	ISBN	84 272 3085 0
Illustrator	None	Cover/Jacket	Pablo Ramírez

Seven White Gates

Foreign Title	Siete Verjas Blancas (Seven White Gates)		
Publisher	Molino	Year/Type	1961 Hardback
Translator	Juan García Guerrero	ISBN	84 272 3028 1
Illustrator	Bertram Prance	Cover/Jacket	Pablo Ramírez

Strangers at Witchend

Foreign Title	Caras Extrañas en Witchend (Strangers at Witchend)		
Publisher	Molino	Year/Type	1973 Hardback
Translator	Ramón Margalef Llambrich	ISBN	84 272 3115 6
Illustrator	Escolano	Cover/Jacket	Badia Camps

Treasure at Amorys FE 57

Foreign Title	Tesoro de Amorys (Treasure of Amorys)		
Publisher	Molino	Year/Type	1969 Hardback
Translator	M L Pol de Ramirez	ISBN	84 272 3101 6
Illustrator	Escolano	Cover/Jacket	Badia Camps

Wings Over Witchend FE 58

Foreign Title	Aventura del árbol de Navidad (Adventure of the Christmas Tree)		
Publisher	Molino	Year/Type	1966 Hardback
Translator	M L Pol de Ramirez	ISBN	84 272 3069 9
Illustrator	Carrillo	Cover/Jacket	Badia Camps
Notes	The original book was not illustrated.		

Wonder Why Book of Exploring a Wood FE 59

Foreign Title	Explorando un Bosque (Exploring a Wood)		
Publisher	Toray	Year/Type	1982 Hardback
Translator	Jaime Elias Cornet	ISBN	84 310 2586 7
Notes	Elsie Wrigley's illustrations are retained.		

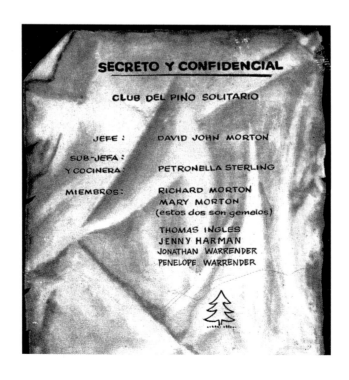

SWEDEN

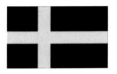

Two Fair Plaits is particularly interesting. It is a rare example of a Malcolm Saville book used as a teaching aid. It is highly abridged, but includes both the English original and Swedish translation.

King of Kings — FE 60

Foreign Title	Konungarnas Konung (King of Kings)		
Publisher	EFS – Forl	Year/Type	1976 Hardback
Translator	Kerstin Hanberger	ISBN	91 7080 3110 0
Notes	As the British edition from Lion except for the translation.		

Mystery at Witchend — FE 61

Foreign Title	Spejarna och Flygplansmysteriet (Spy and Aeroplane Mystery)		
Publisher	Bonnier	Year/Type	1957 Hardback
Translator	Verna Lindberg	ISBN	N/A
Notes	The only illustration is a picture cover by Kerstin Thorvall-Falk.		

Susan, Bill and the Ivy Clad Oak — FE 62

Foreign Title	Susan, Bill och Förrädarna (Susan, Bill and the Traitor)		
Publisher	Svensk Läraretidning	Year/Type	1957 Hardback
Translator	S & C Gripenberg	ISBN	N/A
Notes	Laminated book with cover picture by Maeg Kroon. Contains Ernest Shepard illustrations.		

Susan, Bill and the Wolf Dog — FE 63

Foreign Title	Susan, Bill och Schäfern (Susan, Bill and the Alsatian)		
Publisher	Svensk Läraretidning	Year/Type	1956 Hardback
Translator	Lena Fries	ISBN	N/A
Notes	Laminated book with cover picture by Maeg Kroon. Contains Ernest Shepard illustrations.		

Two Fair Plaits — FE 64

Foreign Title	Two Fair Plaits		
Publisher	Bonniers	Year/Type	1959 Paperback
Translator	Not Stated	ISBN	N/A
Notes	Seven of the original Lunt Roberts illustrations are included.		

USA

It is interesting that both fiction works were published with a change of name and there seems little reason why this should have been done to *The Ambermere Treasure*. Spy in the Hills was the first Malcolm Saville title to be published abroad and is highly collectable.

The Ambermere Treasure — FE 65

Foreign Title	The Secret of the Ambermere Treasure		
Publisher	Criterion Books	Year/Type	1967 Hardback
Translator	N/A	ISBN	N/A
Notes	Marcia Lane Foster's illustrations are included but not her frontispiece. The rather garish cover is not credited. The book appears in various versions due to library re-binding but the standard edition has lime green boards.		

King of Kings — FE 66

Publisher	Our Sunday Visitor	Year/Type	1975 Hardback
Translator	N/A	ISBN	0 87973 694 1
Notes	As the British Lion edition but with purple boards.		

Mystery at Witchend — FE 67

Foreign Title	Spy in the Hills		
Publisher	Farrar & Rinehart	Year/Type	1945 Hardback
Translator	N/A	ISBN	67 11911 (Library of Congress number)
Notes	No text illustrations but cover, a black and white frontispiece and a title page vignette (probably) are by Anne Fleur.		

Wonder Why Book of Exploring the Seashore — FE 68

Publisher	Grosset & Dunlap	Year/Type	1979 Hardback
Translator	N/A	ISBN	0 448 13110 0
Notes	As the British edition but black spine instead of white.		

Wonder Why Book of Wild Flowers Through the Year — FE 69

Publisher	Grosset & Dunlap	Year/Type	1980 Hardback
Translator	N/A	ISBN	0 448 13112 9
Notes	Again, black spine instead of white.		

This bibliography is primarily aimed at listing Malcolm Saville's written work, but we hope you will be interested in some items that have been presented in various media. It was difficult to decide the order in which to list these but we have divided it into those that appeared during his lifetime and those that arrived later, with the odd deviation. They are also in the order that they were produced – almost.

BBC CHILDREN'S HOUR

Many people were introduced to Malcolm Saville's stories when they listened to the BBC's Children's Hour. The importance to a writer of having a story on Children's Hour cannot be overstated and for Malcolm Saville to have his first children's book chosen was astonishing. In fact, *Mystery at Witchend* was published on 1 October 1943 and the serial began exactly one week later.

No recordings of these programmes have surfaced and it was thought that even the scripts had been lost. However, David Schutte has now published the scripts of *Mystery at Witchend*, *Seven White Gates* and *The Gay Dolphin Adventure*.

Some famous names appeared in the early series notably Charles Hawtrey and Harry Fowler who played David and Tom in *Mystery at Witchend*. Peter Mullins has a special place in Malcolm Saville media productions too. He played Dickie in *Mystery at Witchend*, David in both *Seven White Gates* and *The Gay Dolphin Adventure* and Guy Standing in *Redshank's Warning* as well as appearing as Bob Dixon in the film of *Trouble at Townsend*. It is also interesting to see that in two of the serials Dickie was played by a girl.

If you are interested in Children's Hour, we recommend Wallace Grevatt's 1988 book: *BBC Children's Hour A Celebration of those Magical Years*, The Book Guild Ltd (ISBN 0 86332 330 8).

Mystery at Witchend
Four episodes Fridays 8 October – 29 October 1943.
Adapted by Barbara Sleigh.
The cast included Charles Hawtrey as David, Pamela Bevan as Peter, Peter Mullins as Dickie, Patricia Fox as Mary and Harry Fowler as Tom.

The Gay Dolphin Adventure

This serial was broadcast twice, with different casts. The second version had been abbreviated so the episodes were shorter.

Six episodes Fridays 11 January – 15 February 1946.

Six episodes Thursdays 6 October–17 November 1949 (not 10th November).

Adapted by Muriel Levy.

The cast included Peter Mullins (Timothy Harley) as David, Elaine MacNamara (Cavan Malone) as Dickie, Patricia Fox (both versions) as Mary, John Gilpin (Brian Roper) as Jon and Ursula Hirst (both versions) as Penny.

Seven White Gates

Six episodes Fridays 4 October – 8 November 1946.

Adapted by Muriel Levy.

The cast included Peter Mullins as David, Rosamond Barnes as Peter, Elaine MacNamara as Dickie, Patricia Fox as Mary, Michael John as Tom and Dorothy Gordon as Jenny.

On the dustjacket of the fourth edition of the book it states that the story was also broadcast in Holland. As it seems that the BBC series was not recorded, this was presumably in Dutch.

The Riddle of the Painted Box

Two episodes Fridays 12 and 19 October 1948.

Adapted by Muriel Levy.

The cast included Keith Lloyd as Michael and Gillian Andrews as Mary.

Redshanks Warning

Five episodes Thursdays 22 July – 19 August 1948.

Adapted by Muriel Levy.

The cast included Peggy Cameron as Mandy, Dorothy Gordon as Prue, David Page as Tim, Peter Mullins as Guy and John Bishop as Mark.

The Secret of the Hidden Pool

Four episodes Wednesdays 18 November – 9 December 1953 in the West Country only.

Adapted by Honor Wyatt.

Cast details are not known.

The Buckinghams at Ravenswyke

Four episodes Saturdays 28 November – 19 December 1959.

Adapted by Bertha Lonsdale.

The cast included both John Mead and Robert Powell as Charles, Bridget Plummer as Juliet, Christopher Dooley as Simon and Geoffrey Banks as Mr Renislau.

North Home Service

434 m. (692 kc/s) VHF: Holme Moss 93.7 : Douglas 92.8 : Sandale 94.7 : Pontop Pike 92.9 Mc/s

5.0 CHILDREN'S HOUR
'Write Me a Letter'
The Children's Hour
correspondence column of the air
edited and introduced
by Adrian Thomas

5.25 *For Children of Most Ages*
'The Buckinghams at Ravenswyke'
from the book by Malcolm Saville
adapted as a radio serial
by Bertha Lonsdale
1—'The Mysterious Sailor'

Charles Renislau, as a young man,
who tells the story........John Mead
Charles Renislau, as a boy of about
fifteen.....................Robert Powell
Mr. Renislau..............Geoffrey Banks
Mrs. Renislau...........Rosalie Williams
Jan, alias Cartwright, an international
spy.....................Leonard Williams
Juliet Buckingham......Bridget Plummer
Simon Buckingham
Christopher Dooley
Mr. Buckingham..........Ralph Hallett
Mrs. Buckingham.......Madeleine Vacher
Mr. John Marsden......Tom Harrison
Felicity Marsden, his daughter
Helen Fraser
Scene: in and around Whitby
Production by Herbert Smith
See Junior Radio Times

5.55 The Weather
Forecast for land areas, followed by
regional forecasts

6.0 Greenwich Time Signal
NEWS

6.15 NEWS OF THE NORTH

6.20 SPORT SPOTLIGHT
Introduced by George Carr

6.30 (434 m. and all VHF's)
Association Football
A survey of selected matches by Bill
Bothwell, including report on Man-
chester City v. Newcastle United
Other reports include: Everton v.
Manchester United by Bernard
Taylor; Fulham v. Burnley by Bill
Lawndes; Huddersfield Town v.
Liverpool by Douglas Lupton;
Accrington Stanley v. Bury by Jack
Harrison; Workington v. Stockport
County by Peter Cook; and Notting-
ham Forest v. Leeds United;
Brighton and Hove Albion v. Sheffield
United; Newport County v. Halifax
Town

6.42 (434 m. and
VHF Holme Moss only)
Rugby League
A survey of selected matches by Alan
Dixon including Halifax v. Wigan
Other reports on: Wakefield Trinity
v. Australia by Harry Sunderland;
Workington Town v. York by Keith
Macklin; Leeds v. St. Helens by
George Brown; and Hull Kingston
Rovers v. Huddersfield; Salford v.
Barrow

6.55 THOSE WERE THE DAYS
Harry Davidson and his Orchestra
Guest artist,
Ian Blair (baritone)
Introduced by Ivan Samson
Master of Ceremonies,
Charles Crathorn
Produced by Eric Arden
The programme includes: Saunter
Regalia; Naval Threestep
To be repeated on Friday at 12.0

7.15 THE WEEK
IN WESTMINSTER
Lord Balniel, M.P.
gives his impressions of what he
heard and saw in Parliament

7.30 Big Ben
IN TOWN TONIGHT
Chris Howland and Nan Winton
talk to personalities who have
come by land, sea, and air to be
'In Town Tonight'
Edited and produced by Peter Duncan

8.0 Vic Oliver presents
VARIETY PLAYHOUSE
and introduces
Variety Playhouse Orchestra
(Leader, John Jesard)
Conducted by Vic Oliver

TROUBLE AT TOWNSEND FILM

This was a short black and white film (23 minutes), filmed at and around Malcolm Saville's home at Westend Farm in Wheathampstead Hertfordshire. Malcolm Saville was commissioned to write the screenplay.

Often dismissed as a purely instructional film, although it does pack a message about how children should act in the country, it is also designed to entertain. It includes a song and dance routine from its two young stars; David Lees and Petula Clark as Michael and Mary Bishop. Peter Mullins (Dickie Morton on the radio) played Bob Dixon and the adult actors included Thea Wells and Ann Wilton.

Shooting for the film was completed in 1944, but it was not released until January 1946. In the meantime, World War II had come to an end. It is interesting to note that in the book the children's father had been killed, but in the film he comes home in the first scene.

It was produced by Gaumont British Instructional to show at special Saturday morning *Children's Film Club* presentations. This was a new venture from J Arthur Rank and the idea was to produce good quality films that could also be shown in schools and as part of normal film presentations. He had appointed Mary Field to be the general producer of the series and it seems likely that she commissioned the film as she would twelve years later when, as head of the Children's Film Foundation, she would be personally involved with *Treasure at the Mill*.

Though it was clearly not a major film release, it did receive some press coverage, much of it concerned with the series as a whole. British films especially for children seemed to be quite a novelty. *Cinema Magazine* said it was "very good" and praised its "talented juvenile portrayal" and "pleasant scenic backgrounds".

Petula Clark, of course, went on to become a major star. When we spoke to her she remembered that she got very muddy and that her co-star put on weight during the making of the film!

TREASURE AT THE MILL FILM

. . . hundreds of Lone Pine Club members were able to see the World Premiere of

TREASURE at the MILL

in London. If you were unlucky then there is still a chance to see it at the cinemas overleaf—

For the second and last time, Malcolm Saville wrote a book designed to be made into a film. The Children's Film Foundation was now making good quality films, mostly for Saturday morning film shows. CFF's Executive Officer Mary Field knew the artist Harry Pettit who was living with his family in an old mill near Ardleigh in Essex and she thought it would make an ideal location for an adventure film. The Pettit children believe that she originally asked Enid Blyton but it was Malcolm Saville who was commissioned to write the story.

The film was released in January 1957 and starred Richard Palmer as John Adams, John Ruddock as Mr Wilson and Hilda Fenemore as Mrs Adams. The five members of the Pettit family played themselves (though their voices were dubbed) and local people played the other parts. The script was by Mary Cathcart Borer, the producer was A V Curtice and it was directed by Max Anderson. It lasts for 60 minutes, though when it was re-issued in 1974 it had been reduced to 51 minutes.

When we spoke to Richard Palmer he remembered the film with fondness and mentioned that, although he had performed the scene where he shins down a rope from the mill, a stand-in had ridden the horse across the field. Harry Pettit Junior told us that when he had been immersed in the mill run kettles of boiling water had been used to keep him from freezing.

There is a small mystery surrounding this film. All the reference works suggest that it was made in black and white and the Malcolm Saville Society own a copy of this version. However many members are convinced that they have seen a colour version and that the Society showed it at an early Gathering.

TREASURE AND TROUBLE

In 2008, The Malcolm Saville Society released a DVD of the two films based on Malcolm Saville's books: *Trouble at Townsend* and *Treasure at the Mill*. The DVD was made in association with Fougasse Films, whose proprietor, Andy Prada, is a Society member. The result of this collaboration was a high quality, professionally produced DVD.

As well as the two films, there are two short documentaries. In the first, Jeremy Saville, Malcolm's younger son, takes Jenny Aitken around his boyhood home at Westend Farm in Hertfordshire where his father wrote his early books. They show us where Trouble at Townsend was filmed and meet Will Dickinson, whose own father, Bob, was the inspiration for Farmer Dixon in the film.

In the second, Merrilyn Boorman the eldest of the Pettit children who starred in the film talks about the making of *Treasure at the Mill* and visits the locations in Dedham and Ardleigh in Essex. She also makes a poignant return to Spring Valley Mill where the current owner has been fighting a losing battle to save the building from the ravages of time.

The DVD also contains a large number of PDF files with interesting background material on the films, the books on which they were based and the people involved. Additionally, there are many photographs taken at the locations. The DVD is priced at £15 and can be obtained from the Society or from Amazon.

THE AMBERMERE TREASURE TV SERIAL

BBC radio gave a huge fillip to Malcolm Saville's writing career but television must have been a disappointment. ITV was launched in September 1955 but only in the London area so when *The Ambermere Treasure* started in December 1955 only Londoners could see it and, of course, TV sets were still uncommon.

The information on the series is sketchy and we have not seen a recording, or even a still, from the six part series. It started on 27 December 1955 and ran for six twenty minute episodes until 31 January 1956. The story was adapted by Derek Hoddinott and directed by David Eady, both of whom had good careers in TV and film.

We do know that as late as 26 November 1955 the search was still on for an actress to play Mandy. She was eventually played by Gillian Rushen, with Caroline Denzil as Prue and James Doran as Tim. The Standings do not appear in the cast list so may have been edited out.

Though the Jillies were popular, it is surprising that it was not a Lone Pine book that was chosen. Perhaps it was the idea of a story set just outside London that appealed to the producers.

HOME THIS AFTERNOON RADIO PROGRAMME

On 8 January 1970 Malcolm Saville was interviewed by Brian Doyle for this Radio 4 afternoon programme and it was broadcast on 3 February 1970. The series had started in 1964 but only survived for two months after Malcolm Saville's appearance.

SONGS OF PRAISE TV PROGRAMME

Not strictly anything to do with his books but we think it is worth a mention. In December 1976 the BBC programme Songs of Praise came to St. Mary the Virgin Church in Rye. Malcolm Saville had just published *Portrait of Rye* and both he and the illustrator Michael Renton were interviewed for inclusion. It was transmitted on 2 January 1977 (with a repeat on 4 January) and included Malcolm Saville in his garden at Winchelsea talking about his faith.

WITCHEND ONCE MORE RADIO FEATURE

On 19 February 1994 a group of Malcolm Saville enthusiasts set out on a tour of the Lone Pine locations in Shropshire in a vintage bus. On this trip was Chris Eldon-Lee from BBC Radio 4's Kaleidoscope programme, who recorded some of the sounds of the event. This would form the basis of a Kaleidoscope feature broadcast on 2 April 1994 (repeated on 8 April) which also announced the formation of The Malcolm Saville Society, whose founders, Richard Walker and Mark O'Hanlon, were also on the trip.

The Malcolm Saville Society released a recording of the programme on a CD which came as a free gift with the October 2005 edition of *Acksherley!* This also contained two other recordings made for Radio Shropshire about Malcolm Saville. One was called *Witchend Once More* and the other was *A Meeting of the Lone Pine Club* and both were introduced by the Society's co-founder, Richard Walker.

MALCOLM SAVILLE'S
NEWSETTER SCRAPBOOK

HAPPY CHRISTMAS
AND HAPPY READING
from

During the 1970s, Malcolm Saville issued an irregular newsletter to his readers. These can be seen as a bit of a self publicity exercise. This CD ROM was published by Mark O'Hanlon in 2006 priced at £20. It contained all 24 of the newsletters plus some miscellaneous leaflets and letters.

SoundBYTE

In late 2007/early 2008 Mark O'Hanlon launched this audio series in CD format. The idea was that each CD would focus on facets of Malcolm Saville's life and work. The early titles would feature Mark himself being interviewed by Rachel Harrison. Unfortunately, the series ended after only two editions. However, there are five titles since there were two bonus CDs with the first edition and one with the second. Perhaps the most interesting CD is the bonus edition that has a recording of Malcolm Saville addressing a group of children at a South London school in 1980.

CD1	*A Biographical Snapshot*
CD2	*The Long Mynd Shropshire Hill Country*
Bonus CD	*Malcolm Saville's School Visit (July 1980)*
Bonus CD1	*A Passion for Landscape*
Bonus CD2	*Prior's Holt: Farming the real Witchend*

THE SECRET OF THE VILLA ROSA

The Royal National Institute for the Blind publishes audio books for blind and visually impaired people. They have this one Malcolm Saville book in their catalogue (No 2919) and it is available for members to download. The reader is Carol Marsh and the recording lasts for 6 hours and 38 minutes.

It is not uncommon these days for literary characters to begin a new life long after their creator has left us. In children's literature, there have been several sequels to *The Wind in the Willows* and Billy Bunter and The Famous Five have had further adventures. There have been a small number of Malcolm Saville related stories and we have managed to find some space to squeeze them in here.

LITTLE LIGHT

In 2006 Sam Young, a long time Malcolm Saville fan, produced *Little Light*. The original dustjacket announced the story as 'A new Lone Pine story' but a replacement appeared very quickly with this removed and it seems possible there were copyright difficulties.

In fact, the story is not what you would expect. Other authors have taken familiar characters and told new stories about them or, in the case of young characters, imagined them as adults. Sam has written a book where newlyweds Jon and Penny Warrender are visiting the town of Rye for the first time and come across an old copy of *The Gay Dolphin Adventure*. But these are not the Jon and Penny that we know from the Lone Pine stories and neither are the other familiar sounding people that they meet. Or are they? The adventure is in the best Lone Pine tradition and is in a style that Sam imagines Malcolm Saville might have adopted had he decided to write a book for adults.

RICHARD GRIFFITHS Hardback 2006
First Edition 2006 (October)   FO 1

Boards	Blue	Block	Red
Pages	230	Cover price	£18.00
ISBN	978 0-9549069 1 7	Size	19 x 13 cm
Abridged	No	Dustjacket	Anne Proctor
Illustrations	No	Map	Yes
Notes		There are two versions of the dustjacket. The original states that it is a new Lone Pine story. This is omitted from the later version but not from the title page of the book.	

SHORT STORY COMPETITION 2006

The title is a bit of a misnomer for, although The Malcolm Saville Society's competition was launched in 2006, it was not judged until 2007 and the book did not appear until April 2008. All sixteen stories submitted are included and all were based on the Lone Pine characters. The winning entry was *The House by the Needle* by Hélène Wilkinson.

The standard of the entries varied but overall it was very high. The judges were Sam Young, George Jasieniecki and Cathy Elton.

THE MALCOLM SAVILLE SOCIETY Paperback 2008			
First Edition 2008 (April)			**FO 2**
Pages	143	Cover price	(£5.00)
ISBN	978 0 9558714 1 2	Size	25 x 17.5 cm
Abridged	No	Dustjacket	N/A
Illustrations	No	Map	No
Note	The cover has four of Bertram Prance's Lone Pine illustrations.		

SHORT STORY COMPETITION 2009

This time stories on any Malcolm Saville related subjects were allowed and several brought characters from different series together. Another change was that there was a second category: micro stories of less than 500 words. There were sixteen short stories and eleven micro stories.

The judges were Hélène Wilkinson, Tim Hall, Doreen Scott, Liz Manterfield and Mike McGarry and the winners were Jill Howes for her Marston Baines follow-on story *Incident in Tromso* and Nigel Harding for a Lone Pine based micro story *Keep Calm and Carry On*.

THE MALCOLM SAVILLE SOCIETY Paperback 2009			
First Edition 2010 (April)			**FO 3**
Pages	144	Cover price	(£7.00)
ISBN	978 0-9558714 7 4	Size	24 x 17 cm
Abridged	No	Dustjacket	N/A
Illustrations	No	Map	No
Note	The cover has six of Bertram Prance's Lone Pine illustrations.		

ABOUT MALCOLM SAVILLE

Malcolm Saville and his work have been the subject of many articles and even books. During his lifetime these were mostly small pieces often focussing on his current books. To the avid collector there is plenty to find but we have yet to locate anything of a substantial nature. Consequently, we have included here items that have been published in recent years and which are relatively easy to obtain. Of course this book would be an addition to those mentioned here.

ACKSHERLEY!

Acksherley!
No. 44 - Autumn 2009

The Malcolm Saville Society was founded in 1994 and decided to name its members' magazine after an expression often used by the Morton twins in the Lone Pine Books. The first few issues were just photocopied A4 sheets but it has evolved into an A5 booklet which has become more professional in appearance as the years have gone by.

Some of the magazine is taken up with details of the Society's events but there are always articles on various aspects of the author's work, many very well researched. We have dipped into *Acksherley!* often during the compilation of this book.

The magazine is published by the Society three times a year, but is really a quarterly publication because it is supplemented by the Society's programme for its Annual Gathering when the articles tend to be based around the area where the event is held and the books which were located there. An occasional index is provided for members and Acksherley! often has details of books acquired by the Society which are available to members.

BEYOND THE LONE PINE

Mark O'Hanlon is the co-founder of the Malcolm Saville Society and an acknowledged expert on the writer so he was the obvious choice to write a biography of the author.

The story is told in chronological order with details of what was going on both in the subject's personal and business life. Mark was encouraged by the Saville family who provided him with a considerable amount of valuable information in the form of papers and photographs plus their own reminiscences. It makes a fascinating read.

				AM 2
Boards	Blue	Block	Silver	
Pages	206	Cover price	£17.99	
ISBN	0 9528059 3 6	Size	21.5 x 15cm	
Notes	The book is illustrated with black and white photographs and scans of various ephemera.			

BOOK AND MAGAZINE COLLECTOR   AM 3

This little magazine published between 1984 and 2010 was aimed at collectors and could be found in larger newsagents. Each month several writers were featured, usually with a list of their first editions and current values and many booksellers advertised in it.

The first article on Malcolm Saville appeared in the edition for December 1986 (No 33) and was written by Robert Newbury. There is a brief biography and then details of the publication of the books, with information on all the series. It took sixteen years for Malcolm Saville to be featured again but Martin Spence's article in the September 2002 edition (No 222) was again informative and well researched.

THE CLARION   AM 4

This was an occasional short newsletter that The Malcolm Saville Society issued between editions of *Acksherley!*. Before the days of mass internet access it was a way of keeping members up to date. There were seven editions between Spring 2000 and May 2006.

THE COMPLETE LONE PINE

This was Mark O'Hanlon's first book and in it he explored Malcolm Saville's Lone Pine Stories. It was originally published as a paperback and nine years later came the hardback, which had been updated and expanded with more details of the publishing history of the books. Both versions include a preface by Mary Cadogan, original drawings by John C Allsup and David Saville's original Lone Pine maps.

It is in two parts. Mark first tells Malcolm Saville's story, briefly introduces us to the Lone Piners and gives us a synopsis and background details for each book. There are brief details on the characters and places which appear in the books. In the second section, Mark explores the locations where the books were set, pointing out real places and those that were not real. This section is broken down into the six main areas the children visited (London, Shropshire, Sussex, Devon, Suffolk and Yorkshire) and Mark has meticulously researched all of them.

MARK O'HANLON Paperback 1996			
First Edition 1996 (June)			AM 5
Pages	246	Cover price	£9.99
ISBN	0 9528059 0 1	Size	21.5 x 15cm
Second Impression 1996 (August)			
Third Impression 1996 (September)			
Fourth Impression 2001 (April)			
Cover price	£11.99		
Notes	The book is incorrectly described as the second impression.		

MARK O'HANLON Hardback 2005			
Second (revised) Edition 2005			
Pages	309	Cover price	£19.99
ISBN	0 9528059 4 4	Size	21 x 15cm

MALCOLM SAVILLE: A Friendship Remembered

Girls Gone By have been re-publishing the Lone Pine titles for some years so it is not surprising that they should produce a companion volume. This book was an unexpected offering from Viv Turner who knew Malcolm Saville for over 30 years after first contacting him as a child.

She was a super fan really and got to know him well, visiting him many times. He discussed his ideas with her and she suggested some of her own. She wrote quizzes for his newsletters and her main claim to fame is that she compiled the list of Lone Pine characters in the appendix to *Home to Witchend* and receives a warm thank you from the author in his introduction to the book.

This is a warm and unusual book full of anecdotes and photographs and is a perfect complement to Mark O'Hanlon's biography.

GIRLS GONE BY Paperback 2010			
First Edition 2010 (November)			AM 6
Pages	176	Cover price	(£15.00)
ISBN	978 1 84745-095 1	Size	24.6 x 17.4cm

THE WISE OWL

John Allsup is a Malcolm Saville expert and, as an artist, has contributed illustrations for several of Mark O'Hanlon's books. The Wise Owl is an occasional two page newsletter, produced by John that covers news stories in the world of Malcolm Saville. Subjects have included book publications, reports of Malcolm Saville Society events and new discoveries of Malcolm Saville's work. Copies are sent to subscribers or it can be downloaded from John's website.

WEBSITES

There are a number of websites devoted to Malcolm Saville and many more which include him amongst other children's writers. It would be impossible to list all of them but a few that deserve a mention are:

www.witchend.com

The Malcolm Saville Society website is useful for both members and non-members. It previews and reviews Society events and has lots of information about Malcolm Saville and his work. It also has an independent book search facility and lists books for sale.

www.malcolmsaville.co.uk

John Allsup's site is an ongoing encyclopaedia of Malcolm Saville's work and is fully illustrated. It will be the place where updates to this bibliography will be posted in due course.

www.malcolmsaville.com

This is Mark O'Hanlon's site: 'The One Stop Shop for the Malcolm Saville Collector and Enthusiast'. It advertises Mark's books and products - where else can you buy a peewit whistle? It also has links to other Saville sites.

INDEX OF TITLES

MALCOLM SAVILLE DEDICATIONS

The Ambermere Treasure
"To all the boys and girls who have asked me to write a story about hidden treasure."

The Buckinghams at Ravenswyke
"To THEO.A.STEPHENS, O.B.E. who came to Whitby, too."

The Gay Dolphin Adventure
"FOR MY WIFE"

Home to Witchend
"To all Lone Piners of all ages everywhere.
With gratitude for their loyalty through thirty five years."

Jane's Country Year
"For Jane Norris (The Jane I know)"

Lone Pine London
"Dedicated with affection and gratitude
to JEREMY DAVID SAVILLE"

The Luck of Sallowby
"TO MY FRIEND JOCELYN OLIVER who came to Ely too"

Man with Three Fingers
"To the thousands of members of the Lone Pine Club all over the
world who have asked for a story about Tom and Jenny"

Marston Master Spy
"To my wife"

Mystery at Witchend
"FOR TWO R'S AND TWO J'S"

Portrait of Rye
"To the Memory of my Grandfather Rev. Alfred Thomas Saville Missionary
in the South Seas and Minister of Rye Congregational Church 1878-1905"

Redshanks Warning
"To ROSALIND SUSAN OLIVER whose father made me write this book"

The Riddle of the Painted Box
"for Jeremy David"

Saucers over the Moor
"TO ROSEMARY"

The Secret of Grey Walls
"FOR MY WIFE"

The Secret of the Hidden Pool
"For ADELAIDE TUNSTILL who suggested Lyme Regis"

The Secret of the Villa Rosa
"For DOROTHY who came to Orvieto too.
With my love and gratitude."

Seven White Gates
"FOR MY GODCHILD JOANNA MARY"

Strangers at Witchend
"For Alex My Favourite Fan"

All Susan and Bill books
"The 'Susan and Bill' books are dedicated with appreciation to EILEEN
H. COLWELL Children's Librarian Hendon Public Libraries"

Treasure at Amorys
"To All Lone Piners Everywhere"

Trouble at Townsend
"for Susan Jennifer"

Words for All Seasons
"TO MY WIFE"

The dedications shown are those that were included in the first editions. They were often omitted in later editions or occasionally amended. Many of the dedications are to members of Malcolm Saville's family. His wife got five dedications for she is surely the Dorothy in *The Secret of the Villa Rosa*. Malcolm Saville's children were Robin, Rosemary, Jennifer and Jeremy: the two R's and two J's from *Mystery at Witchend*. It is interesting to see that Jeremy got two individual dedications and the girls got one each but Robin, the eldest, did not get one. The Alex who is described as "my favourite fan" is Alex Saville wife of the late Jeremy Saville.

BOOKS IN PRINT

There is nothing more certain to date a bibliography than to list books that are still in print. You can be pretty certain than in the time between a book going to the printer and it hitting the bookshelves some new books will have arrived and others will no longer be available. However we are aware that there is something special in turning the first page of a new book so we are going to give you a list anyway.

Girls Gone By are re-publishing all the Lone Pine books and the most recent are available at their website. Out of stock titles are usually available from book dealers.
www.ggbp.co.uk

RHG Books is run by Richard Griffiths, a former chairman of The Malcolm Saville Society. His beautiful new editions of Home to Witchend and Treasure at the Mill are still in print as is Sam Young's Little Light.
www.rhgbooks.co.uk

Malcolm Saville Online is Mark O'Hanlon's website and you can buy copies of his excellent companion book The Complete Lone Pine and his series of Malcolm Saville CDs.
www.malcolmsaville.com

The Lutterworth Press Words for All Seasons is still available but without the dust-jacket.
www.lutterworth.com

The Malcolm Saville Society still have copies of some of their publications including the Treasure and Trouble DVD, The Flower-show Hat, their Short Story Books and back issues of Acksherley!
www.witchend.com

David Schutte has published three of the scripts of the BBC Children's Hour radio serials and these are still available.
www.davidschutte.co.uk

All of these and a few more can also be obtained at www.amazon.co.uk

NOTES AND AMENDMENTS

In the end there had to be a cut-off point and we acknowledge that there will be errors and omissions in this book, although hopefully not too many. Here is an almost empty page for your notes and please contact us via the Malcolm Saville Society with any additions you are able to let us have. We will publish addendum pages through *Acksherley!* and at www.malcolmsaville.co.uk, John Allsup's Centenary Malcolm Saville website. We also have a dedicated email address at mystery@witchend.com.